The *(unofficial)* *Bridgerton* Book of AFTERNOON TEA

(unofficial)

The Bridgerton Book of
AFTERNOON TEA

OVER 75 SCANDALOUSLY DELICIOUS RECIPES INSPIRED
BY THE CHARACTERS OF THE HIT SHOW

RYLAND PETERS & SMALL
LONDON • NEW YORK

CONTENTS

Introduction

9

A SOCIETY TEA

inspired by Lady Whistledown

46

A LOVESICK TEA

inspired by Penelope Featherington

54

A PARISIAN TEA

inspired by Madame Delacroix

62

A CONFIDANTE'S TEA

inspired by Lady Danbury

70

A TIPSY TEA

inspired by Lord Featherington

78

A FLORAL TEA

inspired by Lady Featherington

86

A FEMINIST TEA

inspired by Eloise Bridgerton

94

A PUNCHY TEA

inspired by Will Mondrich

102

A REBELLIOUS TEA

inspired by Marina Thompson

A BITCHY TEA

inspired by Cressida Cowper

A CURIOUS TEA

inspired by Benedict Bridgerton

A FIRESIDE TEA

inspired by Violet Bridgerton

Afternoon tea with the ton

Are you ravenous for Regency romance? Famished for fun and frolics? Starving for saucy secrets? Do you love sinking your teeth into a sensational scandal? How about sinking your teeth into a sumptuous spread of scones, cakes, macarons, cookies, crostini and other delectable delights fit for a queen, lord, lady or, indeed, Cockney dressmaker posing as a sophisticated Frenchwoman?

Celebrate the drama, deception and – yes – the Duke's derrière by indulging in one of these 16 afternoon teas, each inspired by one of *Bridgerton*'s captivating characters. Recreate Gunter's Tea Shop in your own living room, complete with perfectly pressed tablecloth, three-tiered cake stand and strategically placed spoon in case any of your guests want to recreate the come-hither cutlery-licking scene that caused quite a stir.

The ceremony of afternoon tea became popular amongst the upper-class English in the 1800s, when the Duchess of Bedford plugged her peckishness with an assortment of sweet and savoury snacks to keep her going until dinnertime. What began as a way to keep hunger at bay soon evolved into a social event, where friends would gather in the drawing rooms and manicured gardens of the high society to nibble and natter, dine and discuss, chew and chatter, graze and gossip.

When you throw your own *Bridgerton* afternoon tea, perhaps you'd like to set the scene with a little something extra, depending on which character is 'hosting'. An operatic soundtrack playing at your Opera Tea…

A beautiful bouquet of blooms as a centrepiece to your Floral Tea…
A bar set up in the corner for your Tipsy Tea… A cosy fire crackling
during your Fireside Tea… You could even create your very own
scandal sheet with tantalizing truths about your guests for your
Society Tea (go steady, though – you don't want to lose any friends!).

Each recipe in this book perfectly complements the theme and
character. Only the most refined refreshments will do for Daphne
Bridgerton's Elegant Tea, while diabolically delicious is the order of
the day for smouldering Simon's Gentleman's Tea. Queen Charlotte's
tea is positively eccentric, while Madame Delacroix's is continental-
chic – *ooh la la!* Benedict Bridgerton's Curious Tea serves a suitably
intriguing fare, Eloise Bridgerton's feisty Feminist Tea will inspire you
to burn your corset, Lady Danbury's Confidante's Tea is as badass
as you'd imagine, and Will Mondrich's Punchy Tea really hits the spot.

Each spread is lip-smackingly, mouth-wateringly, tongue-
waggingly wonderful, so prepare yourself for several afternoons
of tempting treats and exquisite eats. Pinkies up.

Brewing the perfect cup of tea

Most of the tea recipes in this book are best made using loose-leaf tea, as it generally produces a better quality tea than tea bags. It's good to keep in mind, as a general rule, that more leaves in the pot will also generally produce a stronger tea. Loose-leaf tea can be steeped several times in order to bring out the best of its flavours. Tea experts often pour an initial amount of hot water into a teapot containing the leaves, and then pour the water out before brewing. This is to wash away any dust on the leaves, and prime them to swell for maximum flavour. Try not to leave the tea leaves in for too long when brewing them (3–4 minutes is usually enough time), as this can create a bad aftertaste.

Brewing and pouring your tea from a teapot is a wonderful way to bring splendour and elegance to an afternoon tea spread. Different teapots can work well for the different teas in this book; delicate white and green teas are best served in pretty china pots, whilst glass pots are a lovely way to watch flowering teas bloom into life. If you're planning on tackling the majority of these inspired tea spreads, perhaps try an all-purpose pot made from not-too-delicate china. Some teapots have built-in infusers, but you can also scoop the tea into a separate infuser, clip to the side of the pot, and then remove it after brewing. Infusers and tea balls are usually made from stainless steel, and make it easy to brew loose-leaf tea whilst keeping the leaves contained. This is the easiest way to make a pot of tea perfect for even the fussiest members of the ton!

AN ELEGANT TEA
inspired by Daphne Bridgerton

Rose congou tea

Teatime crostini

Peach melba scones

Chouquettes

Lemon drizzle cake

Chocolate cherry cake

The 'diamond of the season' is elegance personified. She's dignified, graceful, chaste and, in the words of Queen Charlotte, "Flawless, my dear". She always behaves with the utmost decorum and her curtsies are impeccable. Wait, hang on... Is this the same woman who snorts when she laughs, has a killer right hook and 'gets inappropriate' with the Duke in the garden? While Daphne is, indeed, an exquisite, well-bred beauty, she's also got a tenacious, plucky, saucy side. Like the season's belle of the ball, her afternoon tea is supremely elegant, with a side of sass.

Rose congou tea

The perfect drink for a classic English rose such as Daphne, this sweet, fragrant tea must be served in only the finest china.

5 teaspoons rose congou tea leaves

FOR 1 POT OF TEA

Warm the teapot and add the tea leaves. Pour in slightly cooled boiled water and leave to brew for 3–5 minutes. Pour into cups and serve.

Teatime crostini

Delicate, delectable and downright dreamy, these 'incomparable' nibbles are suitably fit for the Duchess to delight in.

FOR THE CROSTINI TOASTS

1 French-style baguette
olive oil, for brushing

FOR THE PEA & PARMESAN TOPPING

2 tablespoons olive oil
2 shallots, finely chopped
200 g/1½ cups frozen peas
3 tablespoons dry white wine
dried chilli/chile flakes, to taste (optional)
salt and freshly ground black pepper, to season

FOR THE SMOKED SALMON TOPPING

3 tablespoons mayonnaise
½ teaspoon finely grated zest from an unwaxed lemon
3–4 drops of Tabasco or other hot sauce, to taste
100 g/3½ oz. smoked salmon, cut into 12 strips
½ a lemon, for squeezing

fresh dill sprigs, to garnish
Parmesan cheese shavings, to garnish
salt and freshly ground black pepper, to season

a large baking sheet, greased and lined

MAKES 24

Preheat the oven to 190°C (375°F) Gas 5. Cut 24 thin slices of baguette and lightly brush both sides of each one with oil. Arrange on a baking sheet and bake for about 10 minutes, until crisp and golden. Transfer to a wire rack and let cool while you make the toppings.

Heat the oil in a saucepan set over a low heat. Add the shallots and gently sauté for about 3 minutes, until tender and translucent. Add the peas and the wine to the pan. Cover and cook for 3 minutes, until the peas are tender, then tip them into a food processor or blender and blend until smooth. Transfer to

a bowl and season to taste with salt and a pinch of dried chilli flakes, if using.

To assemble the crostini, spoon the pea purée onto 12 crostini toasts, top with Parmesan cheese shavings and serve. Combine the mayonnaise, lemon zest and Tabasco. Spoon lemon mayonnaise onto the other 12 crostini toasts. Top with a strip of smoked salmon and squeeze lemon juice over it. Garnish with a sprig of dill and serve.

Peach melba scones

Daphne's heart almost breaks when Simon refuses to give her what she most desires... but, like these scones, things turn out peachy in the end

100 g/¾ cup self-raising/ self-rising flour

1 teaspoon baking powder

30 g/⅓ cup ground almonds/ almond meal

30 g/2 tablespoons unsalted butter, chilled and cubed

2 teaspoons almond extract

30 g/2 generous tablespoons caster/white granulated sugar, plus extra for sprinkling

2–3 tablespoons milk

TO SERVE

3–4 tablespoons clotted cream or whipped double/heavy cream

1 nectarine, thinly sliced

16 raspberries

3 tablespoons peach preserve

icing/confectioners' sugar, for dusting

a scone cutter (5 cm/2 inch diameter)

a large baking sheet, greased and lined

MAKES 16

Preheat the oven to 180°C (350°F) Gas 4.

Sift the flour and baking powder into a mixing bowl and add the ground almonds. Rub the butter into the flour mixture with your fingertips, until it resembles fine

breadcrumbs. Add 1 teaspoon of the almond extract, the sugar and 2 tablespoons milk and mix to form a soft dough. Add a little more milk if the mixture is too dry.

On a flour dusted surface, use a rolling pin to roll out the scone dough to a thickness of 2 cm/ ¾ inch and stamp out 16 rounds using the cutter. Put the scones on the baking sheet a small distance apart. Using a pastry brush, glaze the tops of the scones with the remaining milk mixed with the remaining

1 teaspoon almond extract. Sprinkle with sugar.

Bake in the preheated oven for 10–15 minutes, until golden brown and the scones sound hollow when you tap them. Let the scones cool on a wire rack then cut each one in half and fill with a little clotted cream, nectarine slices, a few raspberries and a little peach preserve. Replace the tops of the scones and dust with icing sugar to serve. Serve immediately or store in the fridge until needed.

Chouquettes

Whilst the eldest daughter of the Bridgerton brood is undeniably sophisticated, she's also gutsy. Evidenced by the fact that she thinks nothing of riding in-between her dualling-at-dawn brother and (soon-to-be) lover to save the day – then promptly gets thrown from her horse and dusts herself off. These balls of sweet choux pastry have nothing on the ballsy Bridgerton gal.

65 g/½ cup plain/all-purpose flour
50 g/3½ tablespoons unsalted butter, cubed
75 ml/⅓ cup water
75 ml/⅓ cup milk
1 tablespoon caster/superfine sugar
1 tablespoon vanilla bean paste
a pinch of salt
2 eggs
sugar nibs for sprinkling

a piping/pastry bag fitted with a round nozzle/tip
2 large baking sheets, greased and lined

MAKES 45

Sift the flour twice to remove any lumps. Heat the butter in a saucepan with the water, milk, sugar, vanilla bean paste and salt until the butter is melted. Bring to the boil, then quickly add the sifted flour all in one go and remove from the heat.

Beat hard with a wooden spoon or whisk until the dough forms a ball and no longer sticks to the sides of the pan. Leave to cool for about 5 minutes. Whisk the eggs and then beat into the pastry a small amount at a time using a wooden spoon or whisk. The mixture will form a sticky paste which holds its shape when you lift the whisk up.

Preheat the oven to 200ºC (400ºF) Gas 6.

Spoon the choux pastry into the piping/pastry bag and pipe 45 small balls of pastry a small distance apart on the sheets. Using a wet finger, smooth down any peaks.

Top the pastry with sugar nibs. Sprinkle a little water into the bottom of the oven to create steam which will help the choux pastry to rise.

Bake each sheet in the oven for 10 minutes, then reduce the oven temperature to 180ºC (350ºF) Gas 4 and bake for a further 10–15 minutes until the pastry is crisp.

Remove from the oven and cut a small slit in each bun straight away to allow any steam to escape. Serve the buns warm or cold. The chouquettes are best eaten on the day they are made but can be eaten the following day if stored in an airtight container.

Lemon drizzle cake

When Daphne declares her undying love for the dashing Duke after dancing at their end-of-season ball, it's not so much a drizzle falling from the heavens, as a downpour. After they've dried off, they should go inside to warm up with a cuppa and slice of this zingy cake.

175 g/1½ sticks butter, at room temperature

175 g/¾ cup plus 2 tablespoons caster/white granulated sugar

3 eggs

grated zest of 1 lemon

175 g/1⅓ cups self-raising/ self-rising flour, sifted

FOR THE LEMON SYRUP

grated zest and freshly squeezed juice of 1½ lemons

125 g/⅔ cup minus 2 teaspoons caster/superfine sugar

a 20-cm/8-inch, loose-bottomed, square cake pan, greased and lined

Preheat the oven to 180°C (350°F) Gas 4. Put the butter and sugar in a large bowl and beat until pale and creamy. Beat in the eggs one at a time, then stir in the lemon zest and fold in the flour. Spoon the mixture into the prepared cake pan and level the top. Bake in the preheated oven for about 35 minutes, until the cake has risen and is golden.

A skewer inserted in the centre should come out clean. While the cake bakes, make the syrup. Put the lemon juice and sugar in a small saucepan and warm gently, stirring, until the sugar dissolves. Bring to the boil and boil for about 1 minute, then remove from the heat and stir in the grated lemon zest. Set aside until needed.

When the cake is ready, remove it from the oven and prick the top all over using a skewer.

Pour the syrup over it and leave the cake to cool in the pan. Carefully unmould and slice to serve.

Chocolate cherry cake

The young couple enjoy flirtatious banter, dancing together, covert hand-brushing… When Simon unleashes/pops Daphne's passionate side, it's the cherry on the cake of their enviable relationship. Or, in this case, the multiple cherries on this 'take-me-now' cake.

FOR THE MUD CAKE

220 g/7½ oz. dark/bittersweet chocolate

220 g/2 sticks minus 1 tablespoon unsalted butter

2 tablespoons instant coffee granules

160 ml/¾ cup water

125 g/1 cup plain/all-purpose flour

125 g/1 cup self-raising/self-rising flour

40 g/⅓ cup cocoa powder

½ teaspoon bicarbonate of soda/baking soda

480 g/2½ cups caster/white granulated sugar

a pinch of salt

4 eggs

2½ tablespoons vegetable oil

110 ml/scant ½ cup buttermilk

150 g/½ cup black cherry preserve

FOR THE CHOCOLATE BUTTERCREAM

250 g/2 sticks unsalted butter

50 g/6 tablespoons cocoa powder

350 g/3¼ cups icing/confectioners' sugar

FOR THE VANILLA BUTTERCREAM

250 g/2 sticks unsalted butter

2 tablespoons pure vanilla extract

350 g/3¼ cups icing/confectioners' sugar

TO DECORATE

about 80 white chocolate cigarellos

400 g/14 oz. fresh cherries

red edible glitter

2 x 20-cm/8-inch round cake pans, greased and lined

a large serrated knife

a large palette knife

a side scraper

red organza ribbon

SERVES UP TO 20

Preheat your oven to 160°C (325°F) Gas 3.

First, make the mud cake. Melt the chocolate and the butter in a small saucepan with the instant coffee granules and 160 ml/⅔ cup water. Keep the temperature low and stir the mixture occasionally; turn off the heat when only a few small lumps of chocolate remain – these will melt in the heat of the mixture and turning the heat off early prevents burning.

Sift the flours, cocoa powder, bicarbonate of soda and sugar into a bowl and add the salt. Make a small well in the centre and set aside.

Beat the eggs, oil and buttermilk together in a jug/pitcher before tipping this mixture into the dry ingredients and stirring it into a thick paste.

Pour the melted chocolate and butter mixture on top of this paste and fold everything together with a wooden spoon until you have one glossy mixture in the bowl.

Divide your cake mixture between 2 prepared cake pans and bake in the preheated oven for about 40 minutes or until a skewer comes out clean (or with only a few tiny crumbs attached to it). Allow the cakes to cool completely in their pans.

Make the chocolate buttercream. Roughly carve up the butter and beat in a freestanding mixer for 3 minutes until creamy. You can also do this by hand or using a hand-held electric mixer and a large mixing bowl, although you may find that this takes longer. Add cocoa powder and beat in. Once fully incorporated, add 250 g/2⅓ cups of the icing sugar and beat for 1 minute. Then, in a separate bowl, make the vanilla buttercream, repeating the same steps but beating in 2 teaspoons vanilla extract instead of cocoa powder.

Check the consistency of your buttercreams – you are aiming for the texture of thick whipped cream – if it is too runny, add the remaining icing sugar. You will then need to beat the buttercream for a further 5 minutes, until the sugar is completely incorporated.

Now assemble the cake. Begin by levelling off cakes using a serrated knife to remove any peaks from your cakes, then remove them from their pans.

Spread the cut side of one cake with black cherry preserve and the cut side of the other cake with the chocolate buttercream. Sandwich your cakes together so that the preserve and buttercream are in the centre.

Dollop a generous helping of vanilla buttercream onto the top of your cake and, using a large palette knife, spread the buttercream over the top and sides of the cake. Tidy up the edges of your cake by holding the side scraper flush against your work surface and slightly into the buttercream on the side of your cake. Slowly, pull the scraper towards you and you should see the excess buttercream being removed as you work around the cake. You will need to stop and clean off the scraper every now and then to create a smooth finish. Use your scraper to scrape the top edges of the cake in towards the centre to achieve a clean top edge.

Line up your chocolate cigarellos around the edge of your cake, one by one, pressing each cigarello lightly into the buttercream to secure. When you have completely covered the outside of your cake, carefully tie a ribbon around the middle of the cake; this makes the cake look pretty and also helps to keep the cigarellos secure. Rinse your cherries under cold water, then pat dry with paper towels. Whilst still on the towel, take a generous pinch of the red edible glitter and sprinkle this onto your cherries. Once you are content that they are sufficiently glistening, arrange them atop your cake like precious jewels.

AN ECCENTRIC TEA
inspired by Queen Charlotte

Lapsang souchong tea

*'Coronation' chicken sandwiches with
pickled red onion*

Raspberry meringues

Fig & pistachio cupcakes

Spanish windtorte

Attention-grabbing. Extravagant. Theatrical. And that's just her wigs. Queen Charlotte – with her lavish fashion choices, blasé demeanour and ability to make girls faint with a wave of her hand – is unapologetically eccentric. Don't expect this drama queen to serve her afternoon tea with a smile; you're much more likely to be met with a bored expression and assertion of "I want to be entertained". She may also be busy sniffing snuff or spoon-feeding her Pomeranian pups with treats from the table. But what she lacks in charm, dottie Lottie makes up for in wit, flamboyance and audacity.

Lapsang souchong tea

This black, smoky tea is somewhat of an acquired taste. Love it or loathe it, like the magnific monarch, it can't be ignored.

3–4 teaspoons lapsang souchong tea leaves

sugar or honey to taste

milk, as desired

FOR 1 POT OF TEA

Warm the pot and add the tea leaves. Pour over boiling water and leave to brew for 3–5 minutes. Sweeten to taste with sugar or honey and add milk, if desired.

~~~~~~

'Coronation' chicken sandwiches with pickled red onion

Conceived for the banquet of the coronation of Queen Elizabeth II in 1953, serve these sovereign sandwiches at your afternoon tea and you're sure to curry favour with your gratified guests.

1 red onion

2 tablespoons cider or white wine vinegar

1 teaspoon golden caster/white granulated sugar

100 ml/⅓ cup whipping cream

150 g/¾ cup full-fat Greek yogurt

1–2 tablespoons storebought tikka curry paste

1 teaspoon medium curry powder

3 tablespoons mango chutney

juice of ½ a lime

3 cooked chicken breasts

75 g/½ cup sultanas/golden raisins

1 teaspoon nigella or kalonji/ black onion seeds

8 slices of white bread

150 g/1 stick plus 2 tablespoons butter, softened

a handful of fresh coriander/ cilantro leaves

salt and freshly ground black pepper, to season

MAKES 24

Start by lightly pickling the red onion. Peel, half and thinly slice the onion and tip into a bowl. Add the vinegar, sugar and a pinch of salt. Mix well, cover and set aside for 1 hour to allow the onion slices to soften.

In another bowl lightly whip the cream so that it will barely hold a peak. Add the Greek yogurt, storebought tikka curry paste, curry powder, half of the mango chutney and the lime juice. Season with salt and black pepper and mix gently to combine everything.

Shred the chicken breasts and add to the curried yogurt along with the sultanas and the nigella or kalonji seeds. Mix to coat the chicken. Drain the red onion from the pickling liquid. Lay the bread slices out on the work surface and spread with a thin layer of butter, followed by a layer of reserved mango chutney. Divide the chicken mixture between half of the bread slices and top with a pinch of pickled red onion slices. Scatter with fresh coriander leaves and top with the remaining bread slices.

Gently press the sandwiches together and cut into fingers or triangles to serve.

Raspberry meringues

Light, sweet and airy, these meringues are the exact opposite of the brash, bossy and blunt royal. But, like the gossip the quirky queen is so fond of, they're well worth getting stuck into.

6 egg whites

350 g/1¾ cups caster/superfine sugar

150 ml/⅔ cup storebought raspberry coulis, for painting

baking sheets, greased and lined

a pastry brush

MAKES ABOUT 40

Preheat the oven to 110ºC (215ºF) Gas ½.

Pour water into a large saucepan until one third full and heat to simmering point over a medium–low heat.

Put the egg whites and sugar in a wide, shallow metal bowl and lightly mix to combine. Sit the bowl over the pan of simmering water (making sure that the bottom of the bowl doesn't touch the water) and let the mixture heat up until it is warm to the touch and the sugar has dissolved. Stir occasionally.

Remove from the heat and whisk with an electric whisk until glossy and stiff peaks are reached.

Dot a bit of the mixture in each corner of the baking sheets and stick the parchment paper to it.

Using 2 tablespoons, scoop the mixture into golf-ball sized meringues onto the prepared baking sheets.

Bake in the preheated oven for 50–60 minutes until firm. Remove the meringues from the oven. Using a pastry brush, paint raspberry coulis onto the meringues and put back into the oven to bake until the coulis has turned a darker, more purpley

colour and the meringue is dry to the touch. The coulis can feel slightly sticky.

Remove from the oven and let cool. Remove from the parchment paper and store in an airtight container for up to 1 week.

Preheat the oven to 180ºC (350ºF) Gas 4.

Stir the pistachio nuts through the chocolate sponge mixture, then divide the mixture between the paper cases and bake in the preheated oven for 25 minutes, until an inserted cocktail stick/ toothpick comes out clean. Allow to cool in the pan for 10 minutes, then transfer to a wire rack to cool completely. Brush the tops of the cakes with a little honey.

Whisk the mascarpone cheese with the icing sugar and divide between 2 bowls. Stir the purple colouring through one of the bowls to get a mid-shade. Fill one small piping/pastry bag with the white frosting and fill the other with the purple frosting. Mix the Nutella to loosen and use to fill the third small bag. Snip a 1.5-cm/½-inch hole from the end of each and place inside the large disposable piping/pastry bag fitted with a large star nozzle/tip.

Twist the top of the piping/ pastry bag and pipe a swirl on the top of each cake. Decorate each with a fig half, some chopped pistachio nuts and white sugar pearls, then use a soft paintbrush to apply a little gold leaf to each fig, if using. Drizzle with the honey and serve.

Fig & pistachio cupcakes

Nutty, fruity and oh-so kooky, these dark, delectable delights are perfect for Queen Charlotte, who doesn't give a fig what anyone thinks of her.

½ quantity of Double Chocolate Sponge mixture (see page 53)

50 g/generous ⅓ cup pistachio nuts, chopped, plus extra to decorate

4 tablespoons runny honey, plus extra for brushing

525 g/2⅓ cups mascarpone cheese

275 g/2 cups icing/confectioners' sugar

purple gel or paste food colouring

375 g/3¼ cups Nutella

6 fresh figs, halved

1 teaspoon white sugar pearls

4 sheets edible gold leaf (optional)

12-hole muffin pan lined with paper cases

3 small disposable piping/pastry bags

a large disposable piping/pastry bag fitted with a large star nozzle/tip

a soft paintbrush

MAKES 12

Spanish Windtorte

As if there's not already enough to discuss in the ton, this fancy, scene-stealing dessert is the ultimate talking point, and will most certainly be the crowning glory of your elaborate afternoon tea.

FOR THE FIRST MERINGUE

4 egg whites

225 g/generous 1 cup caster/
   superfine sugar

FOR THE SECOND MERINGUE

2 egg whites

115 g/generous ½ cup caster/
   superfine sugar

FOR THE THIRD MERINGUE

4 egg whites

250 g/1¼ cups caster/superfine
   sugar

FOR THE CAKE

115 g/generous ½ cup caster/
   white granulated sugar

115 g/1 stick butter, softened

2 eggs

115 g/¾ cup plus 2 tablespoons
   self-raising/self-rising flour,
   sifted

30 g/⅓ cup unsweetened cocoa
   powder, sifted

2 tablespoons natural/
   plain yogurt

FOR THE FILLING

600 ml/2½ cups heavy/double
   cream

1 tablespoon icing/confectioners'
   sugar, sifted

1 teaspoon pure vanilla extract

400 g/14 oz. cherry compote

TO DECORATE

**sugar flowers, traditionally sugar
   violets or fondant violets**

3 baking sheets, greased and lined

2 piping/pastry bags fitted with
   round nozzle/tip and star
   nozzle/tip

20-cm/8-inch round cake pan,
   greased and lined

SERVES 12

Preheat the oven to 130ºC (250ºF) Gas ½.

For the first meringue, whisk the egg whites to very stiff peaks and then whisk in the caster sugar, a spoonful at a time, until you have a glossy meringue. Spoon the meringue into the piping/pastry bag fitted with the large round nozzle/tip. With the first meringue you need to pipe 2 whole discs of meringue and 4 rings of meringue all of the same size. Draw round an 18-cm/7-inch plate on the underside of the paper and use this as a template for your piping.

Once you have piped the ring of the meringue, carefully remove the plate. You can do this by sliding a knife underneath and, while pressing down firmly on the top of the plate, use the knife to lever the plate up. Don't worry if the plate touches the meringue as it will all be covered with

a further layer of meringue in the next baking stage.

On the 4 meringue rings, pipe a second layer of meringue on top of the rings to make them higher. With the 2 remaining meringues, fill the circle to make discs by piping a spiral of meringue in each, making sure that there are no gaps. You can use 3 large baking sheets and pipe 2 meringues onto each.

Bake the meringues in the oven for about 1–1½ hours until the meringue rings and discs are crisp. If you are baking the sheets of meringue in the oven at the same time, the lower sheets will take longer to cook than the top sheets, depending on the heat of your oven.

Leave the meringues to cool completely. Keep the oven on for the next batch.

For the second meringue, whisk the egg whites to stiff peaks and then, as before, whisk in the caster sugar, a spoonful at a time, until the meringue is smooth and glossy. Pipe 2 flat disks of meringue. Leave one of the flat discs of meringue aside, as you will not need this until the next stage.

Place the other whole disc of meringue into the centre of one of the baking sheets. Taking great care, one by one, lift the meringue rings and place on top of the meringue disc, fixing in place with a little of the second meringue mixture. You want to stack the rings so that they make a casket with the disc on the base as the bottom of the casket. Using the remaining second meringue and a spatula, gently spread a thin layer of meringue over the outside and inside of the sides of the casket so that the individual rings from the first baking are all covered and your casket has smooth sides. If any of the meringue rings break when you lift them, do not worry and simply stick them in place on top of one of the other rings with a little of the second meringue.

Bake in the oven for a further hour or so until the meringue casket is crisp. Remove from the oven and leave to cool. Leave the oven on. The third meringue is a Swiss meringue and is cooked over the heat. Place a large mixing bowl over a pan of simmering water and add the egg whites and sugar together. Whisk all the time until you have a thick meringue mixture. This will take about 5 minutes using an electric whisk (you can use a hand whisk which will take longer and will make your arm hurt!). Remove from the heat and continue to whisk using a stand mixer until the meringue cools. Spoon the meringue into the piping/pastry bag fitted with a star nozzle/tip and pipe rings of stars around the casket and on the reserved second disc, which will act as the lid for the torte. You can be as creative as you want with the meringue decoration and use different shaped nozzles/tips if your piping/pastry bag has an interchangeable fixing. Bake the casket and lid in the oven for about 30 minutes until the Swiss meringue is firm. Leave to cool. Increase the oven temperature to 180ºC (350ºF) Gas 4.

For the cake, whisk together the caster sugar and butter until light and creamy. Add the eggs, one at a time, whisking after each egg is added. Gently fold in the sifted flour, cocoa powder and yogurt. Spoon the cake mixture into the prepared cake pan and bake for 20–25 minutes until the cake is firm and springs back to your touch and a knife comes out clean when inserted into the centre. Leave to cool. Using a sharp knife, trim the cake so that it is just smaller than the size of the cavity of your casket. Cut the cake in half horizontally so that you have 2 discs of cake.

For the filling, in a mixing bowl, whisk the double cream, icing sugar and vanilla to stiff peaks. Now it is time to fill your Windtorte! Lift the Windtorte very carefully to a serving plate or cake stand. Reserve a few spoonfuls of the cream for sticking on the flowers later. Spoon one-third of the cream into the cavity and top with one-third of the cherry compote. Place one of the cakes on top and then cover with another one-third of the cream and another one-third of the cherries. Place the second cake on top and cover with the remaining cream and cherries. Cover the Windtorte with the meringue lid.

Decorate with the sugar flowers, fixing them in place with a little of the reserved cream.

Serve straight away, and be prepared for a fleeting rush of sadness when you cut the cake, destroying all your hard work in a matter of seconds! Any uneaten meringue should be stored in the fridge for 2 days.

AN OPERA TEA

inspired by Siena Rosso

Ginger & honey tea

*Buffalo mozzarella, pickled fig
& lemon crostini*

Fraises-des-bois friands

Cherry & pistachio cupcakes

Opera cake

Despite the torment Siena feels during her clandestine love affair with the conflicted Anthony Bridgerton, this dedicated diva still sings her (breaking) heart out to entertain and enchant her audience. Now you can eat your heart out in her honour with this devastatingly delicious Opera Tea. Delicate mozzarella and fig crostini serve as an amuse-bouche curtain-raiser, while steaming ginger and honey tea is the intermission refreshment, before the gold-flecked opera cake takes centre stage and steals the show. The talented, passionate Siena may have just been upstaged. Bravo!

Ginger & honey tea

All that singing must wreak havoc on Siena's powerful voice. Becoming croaky would be disastrous; this sweet-and-spicy tea will hit the right note by soothing her precious throat.

4 green tea bags, or use the equivalent in tea leaves

5-cm/2-inch piece of fresh ginger root, sliced

a light, flowery honey, such as acacia honey, to taste

FOR 1 POT OF TEA

Warm the teapot and add the green tea and ginger. Fill with boiling water. Give everything a gentle stir and leave to infuse for 4–5 minutes. Sweeten to taste and pour into cups.

Buffalo mozzarella, pickled fig & lemon crostini

The birthplace of opera, Italy is also home to mouth-watering cuisine, including crunchy crostini. After giving Anthony an earful, Siena should take comfort in one (or 20) of these moreish mouthfuls.

FOR THE PICKLED FIGS

400 ml/1¾ cups minus 1 tablespoon rosé wine

100 ml/⅓ cup plus 1 tablespoon sweet raspberry vinegar

1 small fresh red chilli/chile

1 clove

6 dried lavender heads

250 g/2½ cups soft dried figs (about 10), quartered

FOR THE LEMON BUFFALO MOZZARELLA

2–3 tablespoons extra virgin olive oil

grated zest and juice of 1 small lemon

1 teaspoon sea salt crystals

250 g/8 oz. buffalo mozzarella cheese (about 2 balls)

FOR THE CROSTINI

1–2 French-style baguettes, each cut into 1-cm/½-inch slices

2–3 baking sheets

MAKES ABOUT 20

To make the pickled figs, put all the ingredients except the figs in a saucepan and reduce the liquid by half over a medium heat. Remove from the heat, add the figs and allow to cool.

For the mozzarella, pour the olive oil into a bowl and mix with the lemon zest and juice and the salt crystals. Tear the mozzarella cheese in half and in half again, repeating until you have enough pieces to match your fig halves. If the mozzarella cheese is very soft, tear it in half then cut it with scissors. Gently coat the mozzarella cheese in the lemon mixture and leave for 1 hour to infuse.

Preheat the oven to 200°C (400°F) Gas 6. To make the crostini, bake the bread slices on baking sheets in the oven for 10–15 minutes until golden.

To assemble, put a piece of infused mozzarella cheese and a pickled fig quarter on each crostini so they lean against each other. Serve immediately.

Fraises-des-bois friands

Strawberries are often considered the food of love and romance. Translated, 'fraises-des-bois' means 'wild strawberries'. What bite could be more fitting for the wild, loved-up Siena?

70 g/½ cup ground almonds/
  almond meal
30 g/¼ cup plain/all-purpose
  flour
a pinch of salt
120 g icing/confectioners' sugar
100 g/6½ tablespoons butter
3 egg whites
80 g/3 oz. fraises-des-bois or
  chopped fresh strawberries

6 friand moulds, lightly greased

MAKES 6

Preheat the oven to 180°C (350°F) Gas 4.

Mix the almonds, flour, salt and sugar in a large bowl.

Melt the butter in a small saucepan, then remove from the heat and leave to cool. Whisk the egg whites until frothy and light (it's not necessary to whip them into peaks as you would if making meringues).

Trickle the butter into the dry ingredients and add half the egg whites. Mix lightly, and then add the remaining egg whites and continue to mix until they are fully incorporated.

Spoon the mixture into the prepared moulds and scatter the fraises-des-bois over the top. Bake for about 15 minutes or so, until the friands are risen and golden and spring back when pressed lightly.

Serve warm or leave to cool completely.

Cherry & pistachio cupcakes

These wicked and wanton cupcakes have 'forbidden fruit' written all over them. The secret lovers would relish sinking their teeth into one... then each other.

FOR THE VANILLA CAKE MIXTURE

½ vanilla pod/bean

3 eggs

150 g/1 cup icing/confectioners' sugar

150 g/1 cup plus 2 tablespoons plain/all-purpose flour

1 teaspoon baking powder

150 g/1 stick plus 3 tablespoons butter, melted

50 g/½ cup finely chopped pistachios, plus extra to decorate

12 glacé/candied cherries

FOR THE PISTACHIO BUTTERCREAM

180 g/1½ sticks butter, at room temperature

320 g/2¼ cups icing/confectioners' sugar

50 ml/3½ tablespoons milk

1 tablespoon pure vanilla extract

2 tablespoons pistachio paste*

1 tablespoon Kirsch (cherry liqueur)

green food colouring (optional)

a cupcake pan, lined with 12 cupcake cases

a piping/pastry bag, fitted with a star-shaped nozzle/tip

MAKES 12

Make the vanilla cupcake mixture the day before you want to bake the cupcakes. Split the vanilla pod lengthways and scrape the seeds out into a bowl. Add the eggs and sugar and beat with an electric whisk until tripled in volume and the beaters leave a thick ribbon trail when you lift them out of the mixture. Fold in the chopped pistachios. Cover and refrigerate for 24 hours.

The next day, preheat the oven to 160ºC (325ºF) Gas 3.

Divide the mixture between the cupcake cases and bake in the preheated oven for about 15–20 minutes. Remove from the oven and then allow to cool completely.

To make the pistachio buttercream, put the butter, sugar, milk, vanilla extract, pistachio paste and Kirsch in a bowl and beat with an electric whisk or by hand with a wooden spoon until you get a light, fluffy texture. Stir in drops of the food colouring until you get the desired shade of pistachio green, if you like.

Fill the piping/pastry bag with the buttercream and pipe on top of the cold cupcakes.

Balance a glacé cherry on top and sprinkle extra chopped pistachios around the edge.

*To make your own pistachio paste, roast 125 g/1 cup pistachios on a baking sheet in a preheated oven at 160°C (325°F) Gas 3 for 10 minutes, taking care not to let them burn. Transfer to a bowl. Put 175 ml/⅔ cup water and 60 g/⅓ cup caster/superfine sugar in a saucepan and bring to the boil. When the sugar has dissolved and the liquid is boiling, cook over a medium heat for 5 minutes. Carefully pour this syrup into a food processor with the roasted pistachios and 30 g/⅓ cup ground almonds and pulse until you achieve a smooth paste. Use this as directed in the main recipe.

Opera cake

What a performance! Rest assured, the effort you put into this dramatic cake will be well worth it – your guests will be crying out for an encore!

1 tablespoon caster/superfine sugar dissolved in 150 ml/ ⅔ cup espresso coffee

50 g/1½ oz. dark/bittersweet chocolate, melted

150 ml/⅔ cup Frangelico (hazelnut liqueur)

a little gold leaf, to decorate

FOR THE HAZELNUT JOCONDE

2 eggs plus 2 egg yolks and 5 whites

175 g/1½ cups icing/ confectioners' sugar, sifted

175 g/1¼ cups ground hazelnuts

40 g/3 tablespoons butter, melted

50 g/⅓ cup plus 1 tablespoon plain/all-purpose flour, sifted

a pinch of salt

50 g/¼ cup caster/superfine sugar

FOR THE FRENCH BUTTERCREAM

200 g/1 cup caster/white granulated sugar

3 egg yolks, whisked

200 g/1 stick plus 5 tablespoons softened butter

2 tablespoons Frangelico (hazelnut liqueur)

FOR THE GANACHE

250 g/8 oz. dark/bittersweet chocolate, chopped

250 ml/1 cup single/light cream

25 g/2 tablespoons butter

two 38 x 25-cm/15 x 10-inch roulade pans, greased and lined

a sugar thermometer

SERVES 12–15

Preheat the oven to 180°C (350°F) Gas 4.

First, make the joconde. Whisk the eggs, egg yolks and icing sugar together until pale and fluffy. Add the ground hazelnuts and continue whisking for about 5 minutes. Stir in the melted butter and flour until thoroughly mixed. In a separate and clean bowl, whisk the egg whites and salt until stiff, but not dry. Whisk in the caster sugar in two stages and continue whisking until the meringue is stiff and glossy. Add a third of the meringue to the nut mixture and vigorously stir in to slacken the batter. Fold in the remaining meringue and pour the mixture into the prepared cake pans. Use a palette knife to smooth the mixture out thinly. Bake in the preheated oven for 8–12 minutes, or until the Joconde is no longer sticky to touch. Remove from the oven and leave to cool in its pan on top of a wire rack for about 10 minutes before turning onto the rack to cool.

To make the French buttercream, put the sugar and 2 tablespoons of water in a pan set over a gentle heat. Stir until the sugar has dissolved. Increase the heat slightly and simmer until it reaches the soft ball stage – this happens at 113°C (235°F).

Put the whisked egg yolks in a bowl and trickle the hot syrup in, whisking all the time. Once pale and fluffy, leave to cool a little before whisking in the butter. Whisk in the liqueur and leave to cool until ready to use.

To make the chocolate ganache, heat the cream to just boiling point in a pan set over a gentle heat. Pour the hot cream over the chocolate in a heatproof bowl and mix with a spatula until smooth and glossy. Whisk in the butter at the end before cooling.

To assemble, trim the sheets of joconde into rectangles, cut each one in half so that you have 4 pieces. Turn a piece over and paint with the melted chocolate. Let set at room temperature before turning it over. Apply a liberal amount of the espresso to the top. Evenly spread a layer of buttercream about 5 mm/ ¼ inch thick over the brown espresso-soaked sponge and place another layer of joconde on top. Soak the cake in hazelnut liqueur. Spread a thin, even layer of ganache over the top. Leave to set at room temperature. Top with a third layer of joconde and soak with more espresso. Finish with a layer of buttercream before placing the final joconde on top. Soak in hazelnut liqueur and top with more ganache. Set at room temperature. Decorate with a little gold leaf, trim the edges and serve.

A GENTLEMAN'S TEA
inspired by *The Duke of Hastings*

Yunnan tea

Boiled eggs with asparagus 'dippers'

Smoked mackerel pâté on toast

Drop scones with cinnamon butter

Rich fruit cake

Can't you just picture the devilishly debonair Duke sitting down to dine here? Daphne is opposite him, watching with lusty eyes as the cinnamon butter slowly melts into his drop scones, he sultrily spreads his smoked mackerel pâté onto his toast, then bites down into his crumbling fruit cake, before finally dipping his firm asparagus into the boiled egg. *Swoon!* As Daphne sees the yolk trickle over the side, desire floods her and she joins her husband on his side of the table... The tea goes cold.

Yunnan tea

From the roaring fire as a backdrop to their wedding night to their 'I burn for you' declarations, the relationship between Daphne and the Duke made us all hot under the collar. This smoky, peppery tea will add to the steaminess and really hit the spot.

3–4 teaspoons Yunnan tea leaves
sugar or honey, to taste
milk, to taste

FOR 1 POT OF TEA

Warm the pot and add the tea leaves. Pour in the boiling water, stir and leave to brew for 3–4 minutes. Add milk as desired and sweeten to taste with sugar or honey.

Boiled eggs with asparagus 'dippers'

Not that the virile duke needs any extra encouragement but, due to the vitamin E and folate found in asparagus, it's known to be an aphrodisiac. Which could inspire him to pose the question to his eager wife, 'How do you like your eggs in the morning, darling?' Get dipping, sir!

2 eggs
150 g/5½ oz. fresh asparagus, trimmed
salt and freshly ground black pepper, to season

SERVES 2

Place the eggs in a saucepan of water and simmer for 3–4 minutes only. Drain and place in egg cups. Meanwhile, fill a frying pan/skillet with salted boiling water to a depth of about 3 cm/1¼ inch. Add the asparagus and blanch for about 3 minutes, until just tender.

Drain the asparagus well and pat dry on paper towels.

To serve, carefully slice the tops off the eggs. Serve with the asparagus spears on the side for dipping into the runny yolks and provide little dishes of salt and black pepper to season.

Smoked mackerel pâté on toast

Although he was reluctant (to say the least) at first, Simon eventually got on board with producing an heir. Oily fish like mackerel would have helped his 'little swimmers' become as strong as they could be.

200 g/7 oz. smoked mackerel fillets, skinned

120 g/½ cup plus 1 tablespoon mascarpone cheese

a pinch of freshly grated nutmeg

juice of ½ a lemon

thin slices of toasted granary bread, to serve

salt and freshly ground black pepper, to season

SERVES 4

Put the mackerel fillets in a bowl and use a fork to flake them.

Transfer to a food processor and add the mascarpone, nutmeg, a little lemon juice and a good grinding of pepper. Blend to make a smooth pâté, then stir in more lemon juice to taste.

Spoon the pâté into 4 small ramekins, or a single serving dish, and serve with plenty of hot granary toast on the side.

To make the cinnamon butter, beat together the butter, icing sugar and cinnamon until smooth and creamy. Either spoon the butter into a small dish and level the top, or wrap it in clingfilm/plastic wrap and shape into a log that can be chilled until firm and sliced into rounds to serve.

To make the drop scones, put the flour and sugar in a bowl and mix to combine. Make a well in the centre. Add the egg and half the milk, and gradually work in the flour to make a smooth batter. Beat in the remaining milk.

Set a large, non-stick frying pan/skillet over a low heat. Brush the hot pan/skillet with oil, then wipe off any excess oil using paper towels.

Drop tablespoonfuls of batter into the pan/skillet and cook for 1–2 minutes, until bubbles appear on the surface.

Flip over each drop scone and cook for a further 30–60 seconds until golden. Keep the cooked scones warm as you go.

Serve warm with generous pats of the cinnamon butter for spreading.

Drop scones with cinnamon butter

The brooding, damaged Duke arrived on our screens with a heart of stone but, like the golden butter trickling down this stack of drop scones, it was soon melted by the love of a good woman.

115 g/¾ cup plus 2 tablespoons self-raising/self-rising flour

1 tablespoon caster/white granulated sugar

1 egg, beaten

150 ml/⅔ cup full-fat/whole milk

vegetable oil, for brushing

FOR THE CINNAMON BUTTER

85 g/6 tablespoons butter, at room temperature

4 teaspoons icing/confectioners' sugar

½ teaspoon ground cinnamon

MAKES ABOUT 20

Rich fruit cake

Simon Basset is a complicated suitor with many layers. A 'simple sponge' man he ain't! The raisins, figs and apricots in this cake combine for a flavour so gratifying, it's enough to gladden even the most mystifying of men.

175 g/1½ sticks butter

100 g/½ cup caster/white granulated sugar

50 g/¼ cup light brown sugar

3 eggs

grated zest of 1 unwaxed orange

200 g/1½ cups self-raising/self-rising flour

1 teaspoon baking powder

2 tablespoons brandy

200 g/7 oz. mixed dried vine fruits

50 g/⅓ cup dried figs, chopped

100 g/¾ cup dried apricots, chopped

50 g/⅓ cup glacé/candied cherries, halved

50 g/½ cup minus 1 tablespoon blanched almonds

an 18-cm/7-inch cake pan, greased and lined

SERVES 6–12

Preheat the oven to 160°C (325°F) Gas 3.

Put the butter and sugar in a bowl and beat until fluffy. Beat in the eggs one at a time. Stir in the orange zest, then sift in the flour and baking powder. Mix well to combine. Stir in the brandy, followed by the fruit. Tip the mixture into the prepared pan and spread it out evenly.

Arrange the almonds on top in concentric circles. Bake for about 1 hour 10 minutes, until a dark, golden colour and a skewer inserted in the centre comes out clean. Leave to cool in the pan for about 20 minutes, then turn out on to a wire rack to cool completely. Wrap in foil, and store in an airtight container until ready to slice and serve.

A SOCIETY TEA
inspired by Lady Whistledown

Champagne cocktails

Rosemary & Asiago arancini

Praline cookies

Kiss & tell tarts

Fallen fruit chocolate cake

Dearest Readers,

This author is reliably informed that the only thing you love more than a sordid secret is a tantalizing mélange of fancies to feast on. It is my greatest pleasure to cordially invite you to dine on my Society Tea. Expect only the most notable of nibbles, bites abuzz with flavour, and a cake so intricate even I am lost for words. All will be washed down with the finest Champagne and whisperings of delicious gossip. Rest assured, your appetite for salacious scandal and fanciful food will be satisfied.

Yours truly, Lady Whistledown

Champagne cocktails

Wet your Whistledown with this elegant cocktail. The ton's cryptic columnist fizzes with excitement when revealing the affairs of others; the only thing she likes more than inspiring gasps is toasting the happiness of couples who find their perfect match. Clink!

6 white sugar cubes

Angostura bitters, to taste

brandy, to taste

a bottle of chilled Champagne

6 twists of lemon zest, to garnish

SERVES 6

Put 1 sugar cube in the bottom 6 flute glasses and add 3 drops of Angostura bitters to each. Add a splash of brandy (about 1 teaspoon is fine). Top up with the chilled Champagne and garnish with a twist of lemon. Serve immediately.

Rosemary & Asiago arancini

The ton's social season's calendar is filled with lavish balls where debutantes aim to fill their dance cards with eligible admirers. These risotto rounds are an entirely different type of lavish ball, but still with admirers aplenty.

800–850 ml/3¼–3½ cups vegetable stock

3 tablespoons olive oil

1 white onion, chopped

70 g/4½ tablespoons butter

400 g/2½ cups risotto rice

120 ml/½ cup white wine

100 g/1½ cups finely grated Parmesan cheese

2 tablespoons finely chopped fresh rosemary

200 g/7 oz. Asiago cheese (or other mild Italian cheese), cut into 1-cm/⅜-inch cubes

50 g/⅓ cups fine quick-cook polenta

1 litre/4 cups vegetable oil

FOR THE PASTELLA

1 egg white

30 ml/2 tablespoons sparkling water

30 g/⅓ cup self-raising/self-rising flour

MAKES ABOUT 24

To make the risotto, heat the stock in a saucepan until very hot but not boiling. Heat the olive oil in a frying pan/skillet over a low–medium heat and sauté the onion gently for 10 minutes or so, until soft but not coloured. Add 20 g/1⅓ tablespoons of the butter to the pan and pour in the rice. Stir gently until all the rice grains are shiny and coated in butter. Add the wine, and stir until it has been absorbed. Add the stock, a ladle at a time, stirring gently in between each addition, until the rice is cooked and the stock has all been absorbed. Stir in the remaining butter, the Parmesan cheese and the chopped rosemary. Leave the risotto until completely cold. It helps to make the risotto several hours in advance, or even the day before – you can speed up the cooling process by spreading the risotto onto a baking sheet.

To make the pastella, whisk the egg white, stir in the sparkling water, then add the flour and stir until the mixture is smooth.

Form the rice into balls the size of a large walnut, and push a cube of Asiago cheese into the centre of each one. Roll the arancini in the pastella, then coat lightly with the polenta.

Heat the vegetable oil in a deep saucepan and fry the arancini for 2–3 minutes, until golden. Drain on paper towels and serve immediately, whilst hot.

Praline cookies

With the revelations in her anonymous scandal sheet, Lady Whistledown gives the Regency's high society a lot to chew on. With these sweet, chomp-worthy cookies, she gives them even more.

110 g/1 stick butter, at room temperature and chopped

90 g/½ cup caster/white granulated sugar

40 g/3½ tablespoons muscovado/ light brown sugar

1 teaspoon pure vanilla extract

1 teaspoon single/light cream

1 egg

190 g/1½ cups plain/all-purpose flour

½ teaspoon baking powder

¼ teaspoon salt

90 g/½ cup milk/semisweet chocolate chips

40 g/2½ tablespoons almond praline paste (if you can't find it, use Nutella)

1–2 baking sheets, greased and lined

MAKES ABOUT 25

Put the butter in a bowl and beat with a wooden spoon until very soft. Beat in the sugars until well incorporated and creamy, then add the vanilla extract, cream and egg and beat in. Gradually sift in the flour, baking powder and salt and mix until combined. Finally, mix in the chocolate chips and almond praline paste.

Cover and refrigerate for 30 minutes.

Preheat the oven to 170ºC (325ºF) Gas 3.

Remove the bowl from the fridge. Lightly flour a clean work surface and roll the chilled dough out into a sausage roughly 30 cm/ 12 inch long. Cut the dough into about 25 equal slices and arrange on the prepared baking sheets.

Bake in the preheated oven for about 15–20 minutes until golden brown. Allow the cookies to cool on the baking sheets for 5 minutes, then transfer to a wire rack to finish cooling. Store in an airtight container until ready to serve.

Kiss & tell tarts

The gossipmonger hiding behind her quill describes the heart as 'the most curious of instruments'. These fruity, boozy, crumbly heart tarts are the most curious of confections.

FOR THE SHORTCRUST PASTRY

225 g/1¾ cups plain/all-purpose flour (plus extra for dusting)

100 g/6½ tablespoons unsalted butter, chilled and cubed

½ teaspoon salt

100 ml/6½ tablespoons ice cold water

FOR THE FILLING

100 g/⅔ cup dried cranberries

125 ml/½ cup vodka

125 ml/½ cup Amaretto (almond liqueur)

3 tablespoons orange preserve or thin-shred marmalade

100 g/3½ oz. clementines, peeled and roughly chopped

100 g/¾ cup fresh cranberries

150 g/5½ oz. amaretti cookies, crumbled

TO SERVE

ground cinnamon, to dust

vanilla ice cream

4 heart-shaped tart pans

baking beans

SERVES 4

Put the dried cranberries for the filling in a bowl, pour over 50 ml/3½ tablespoons of vodka and 50 ml/3½ tablespoons of amaretto and leave to rehydrate for at least 2 hours.

Put the flour, butter and salt in a large mixing bowl and gently rub them between your fingers until the texture resembles fine breadcrumbs. Drop by drop, slowly add enough of the cold water to make a stiff dough then bring the dough together with your fingers. Wrap the pastry in clingfilm/plastic wrap and let it rest in the fridge for about 20–30 minutes.

Put 2 tablespoons of the orange preserve in a saucepan with the remaining vodka and amaretto. Gently warm through so that the preserve becomes runny. Add the clementines, fresh cranberries and the strained rehydrated cranberries. Simmer over a low heat and keep stirring for around 10 minutes, then set aside to cool.

Preheat the oven to 180ºC (350ºF) Gas 4.

Remove the pastry from the fridge. On a lightly floured surface, roll it out to 5 mm/¼ inch thick and use it to line the tart pans. Prick the bottom of each pastry case, line with parchment paper and fill with baking beans. Bake the cases in the preheated oven for about 15–20 minutes, then take them out of the oven and remove the parchment paper and baking beans.

Spread a little of the remaining orange preserve over the base of each pastry case. With a slotted spoon, fill the cases with the cooked fruit mixture, dividing it equally between the pans. Be careful not to add too much liquid. Sprinkle the crumbled amaretto cookies over the top, then return to the oven for a final 5 minutes.

Dust the tarts with cinnamon and serve warm, topped with a scoop of vanilla ice cream.

Fallen fruit chocolate cake

Lady Whistledown is cleverly hiding in plain sight – much like the colourful fruit slices on this cake, masquerading as decorative flowers.

250 g/2¼ sticks butter, softened and cubed

500 g/3½ cups icing/confectioners' sugar, sifted

3–5 walnut halves

fresh blackberries, to decorate

edible gold spray

4 sheets of edible gold leaf (optional)

2 figs, 1 halved, 1 quartered

3–5 physalis

3 Gala apples

3 pears

orange, red, purple and green gel or paste food colouring

FOR THE DOUBLE CHOCOLATE SPONGE

450 g/3½ scant cups self-raising/self-rising flour plus 2 teaspoons bicarbonate of soda, sifted (omit soda if baking with US flours)

3 tablespoons unsweetened cocoa powder, mixed with 4 teaspoons just-boiled water

500 g/2½ cups caster/superfine sugar

240 g/2¼ sticks butter, melted and cooled, plus extra for greasing

300 ml/1¼ cups buttermilk

4 eggs

1 teaspoon pure vanilla extract

150 g/5½ oz. dark/bittersweet chocolate, melted

2–3 large baking sheets, greased and lined

three 18-cm/7-inch diameter cake pans, greased and lined

a paintbrush

2 wooden skewers

SERVES 22

Preheat the oven to 180°C (350°F) Gas 4.

Place all the ingredients for the double chocolate sponge in a large bowl and beat with an electric hand whisk until combined and smooth. Transfer to the cake pans. Bake for about 40 minutes, until an inserted cocktail stick/toothpick comes out clean, then allow to cool.

To make the buttercream, use an electric hand whisk to beat the butter until light and creamy. Add a tablespoon of water and gradually whisk in the icing sugar in manageable batches, until smooth and spreadable.

For the apple and pear crisps, preheat the oven to 80°C (160°F) Gas ¼. Slice the apples widthways and the pears lengthways with a mandoline to get thin slices. Flick out any seeds, then arrange the slices on the baking sheets. Bake for 1½ hours or until dried out.

Fill 4 small bowls with 1 cm/⅜ inch of water. Add a little of each of the food colourings to each of the bowls to get the 4 different colours. Use the paintbrush to brush the dried apple and pear slices with the colours.

Return the coloured fruit to the oven for a further 30 minutes to dry. Remove from the oven and leave to cool on a wire rack.

Sandwich the cakes together using 300 g/10½ oz. of the buttercream – the bottom side of the top cake should be facing up. Place the cake on a serving plate or cake board. Crumb-coat the cake using the remaining icing. This will be your final coating giving it a semi-naked look, so scrape off enough icing to reveal some of the sponge.

Spray the walnut halves and some of the blackberries with gold spray, then decorate using some edible gold leaf (if using). Set aside to dry.

Break the skewers into different heights and insert into the top of the cake with the points facing up. Push some of the figs and/or the physalis onto the skewers so that they stand upright and piled one on top of another. Position the fruit crisps to the side and on top of the cake.

Add the blackberries and walnuts, along with remaining figs/physalis. Decorate the figs with the remaining gold leaf. Spray the cake with gold spray.

A LOVESICK TEA
inspired by Penelope Featherington

Moroccan mint tea

Baby rarebits with beetroot & orange relish

Bijoux blondies

Love heart sugar cookies

Heart choux buns

Mini ice cream cakes

A hopeless romantic, poor Penelope finds her romantic situation to be, well, hopeless. Secretly and madly in love with her best friend's brother, Colin Bridgerton, she watches, forlorn, as he proposes to another woman. Although firmly in the 'friend zone', the youngest Featherington still dreams of ending up with the object of her desire. As he leaves to travel the world, however, that's looking increasingly unlikely, so what does pining Pen need to nurse her wounded heart? Chocolate. Ice cream. Cookies. She'll soon find she's more sweet on these treats than the oblivious Mr B.

Moroccan mint tea

Will Colin swing by Morocco on his travels? If he does, he should really pick up some fresh mint tea for his good friend. It's the least he can do, given the amount of heartache he's unwittingly caused her.

2 teaspoons green tea leaves
a handful of fresh mint leaves

FOR 1 POT OF TEA

Warm a teapot. Add the tea and mint leaves and fill with boiling water. Allow to brew for about 3 minutes. Remove the mint and pour into cups.

Baby rarebits with beetroot/beet & orange relish

While she longs to ride off into the sunset with the man of her dreams, for now, Penelope will have to seek solace in this scrumptious sunset-coloured relish. There are worse consolation prizes.

1 small French-style baguette
3 tablespoons white wine
100 g/1 cup plus 2 tablespoons Cheddar cheese, grated
1 teaspoon Dijon mustard
2 egg yolks
fresh dill sprigs, to garnish
salt and freshly ground black pepper, to season

FOR THE BEETROOT/BEET & ORANGE RELISH

1 tablespoon olive oil
1 shallot, finely chopped
1 teaspoon grated fresh ginger
seeds of 2 cardamom pods, crushed
1 raw beetroot/beet, peeled and grated
¼ cooking apple, peeled, cored and grated
juice of 1 orange

To make the beetroot/beet and orange relish, heat the olive oil in a frying pan/skillet and gently fry the shallot for about 3 minutes. Add the ginger and cardamom seeds and fry for another minute. Add the beetroot/beet, apple and orange juice, and season well with salt and pepper. Cook very gently, stirring frequently, for about 20 minutes until tender and moist, but not wet. Check and adjust the seasoning, if necessary, then set aside.

Cut 12 thin slices of baguette on the diagonal, about 1 cm/⅜ inch. Put the wine, cheese and mustard in a small saucepan and heat gently, until the cheese has melted. Season with black pepper, beat in the egg yolks and set aside.

Grill the slices of baguette on one side until golden. Turn over, spoon on the cheese mixture and grill for another 2–3 minutes until golden and bubbling.

Transfer to a serving plate, top with the relish, sprinkle with dill sprigs and serve immediately.

Bijoux blondies

Canary, corn, lemon, daffodil, bumblebee... It seems there isn't a shade of yellow that Penelope hasn't modelled. Whilst she'd undoubtedly find these cake bars delectable, she may declare, 'Not yellow enough, I think.'

250 g/9 oz. white chocolate, chopped

120 g/1 stick butter, chopped

½ tablespoon extra virgin olive oil

4 eggs

140 g/¾ cup caster/white granulated sugar

90 g/⅔ cup plain/all-purpose flour

70 g/½ cup blanched almonds, chopped

FOR THE WHITE CHOCOLATE & OLIVE OIL GANACHE

1 vanilla pod/bean

90 ml/⅓ cup single/light cream

180 g/6½ oz. white chocolate, chopped

40 ml/3 tablespoons mild and sweet extra virgin olive oil

blanched almonds, to decorate

a 20-cm/8-inch square baking pan, greased and dusted with flour

MAKES 6–8

Preheat the oven to 170°C (325°F) Gas 3.

Put the white chocolate and butter in a heatproof bowl set over a saucepan of barely simmering water. Do not let the base of the bowl touch the water. Allow to melt, stirring occasionally, until completely smooth. Stir in the olive oil. Remove from the heat.

In a separate bowl, whisk the eggs and sugar for 1–2 minutes. Sift in the flour and whisk again to mix. Pour the chocolate mixture in and mix well with a wooden spoon. Finally, stir in the chopped almonds.

Spoon the mixture into the prepared baking pan, spread level with a spatula and bake in the preheated oven for about 20 minutes. Allow to cool completely in the pan.

To make the white chocolate and olive oil ganache, split the vanilla bean lengthways and scrape the seeds out into a saucepan. Add the cream and gently bring to the boil.

Meanwhile, put the chocolate in a heatproof bowl set over a saucepan of barely simmering water. (Do not let the base of the bowl touch the water.) Allow to melt, stirring occasionally, until completely smooth. Add the olive oil and stir in. Remove from the heat and pour in the boiled cream. Beat with an electric whisk until smooth and glossy. Spread the ganache evenly over the cold brownie in the pan and refrigerate overnight.

When you are ready to serve, cut the brownie into equal portions and decorate each one with a blanched almond.

Love heart sugar cookies

Although the infatuated Penelope daren't reveal her true feelings to Colin for fear of rejection, perhaps she should whip up a batch of these cookies and anonymously leave them on his doorstep with the note, 'Sweet hearts for my sweetheart'.

115 g/1 stick butter, at room
  temperature
50 g/¼ cup caster/white
  granulated sugar
1 egg yolk
175 g/1⅓ cups plain/all-purpose
  flour

TO DECORATE

1 tablespoon granulated sugar
red food colouring
75 g/2½ oz. white chocolate

2 baking sheets, greased and lined
a heart-shaped cookie cutter,
  6.5-cm/2½-inch diameter

MAKES ABOUT 20

Put the butter and sugar in a bowl and beat until pale and creamy. Beat in the egg yolk. Stir in the flour, then knead the mixture gently to make a soft dough. Wrap in clingfilm/plastic wrap and chill in the fridge for about 30 minutes.

Preheat the oven to 180°C (350°F) Gas 4.

Gently roll out the dough on a lightly floured surface to a thickness of about 4 mm/⅛ inch. Stamp out shapes using the cookie cutter and arrange them on the prepared baking sheets. Re-roll the trimmings to cut out more cookies. Bake for about 10 minutes, until a pale golden colour. Leave the cookies on the baking sheets to cool for a few minutes then transfer to a wire rack to cool.

To decorate, put the sugar in a bowl and add a few drops of food colouring. Work the colouring into the sugar until evenly coloured and pink.

Melt the chocolate in a heatproof bowl set over a pan of gently simmering water. Drizzle lines of chocolate around the outside edge of each cookie. Sprinkle with pink sugar and leave to set before serving.

Heart choux buns

Unrequited love is the worst! While shy Penelope feels invisible, her heart is as delicate as these glazed pastries, and the love triangle she finds herself in with Colin and Marina is just as sticky!

CHOUX PASTRY

65 g/½ cup plain/all-purpose flour

50 g/3½ tablespoons butter, cubed

75 ml/5 tablespoons milk and 75 ml/5 tablespoons water or just 150 ml/5 fl. oz. water

1 teaspoon caster/white granulated sugar

a pinch of salt

2 eggs

FOR THE SUGAR GLAZE

180 g/1½ cups icing/confectioners' sugar, sifted

1 teaspoon pure vanilla extract

pink food colouring

sugar flowers, to decorate

FOR THE MARSHMALLOW FILLING

200 g/1¾ cups icing/confectioners' sugar, sifted

1 tablespoon butter, softened

3 tablespoons marshmallow fluff

1 tablespoon milk

2 baking sheets, lined and greased

2 piping/pastry bags fitted with round nozzles/tips

MAKES 14

First, make the choux pastry. Sift the flour onto a sheet of parchment paper twice to remove any lumps and to add as much air as possible. Heat the butter in a saucepan with the milk and water (or just water), sugar and salt until the butter is melted. As soon as the butter has melted, remove the pan from the heat and quickly add the sifted flour all in one go. (It is important not to let the water heat for longer than it takes to melt the butter as this will evaporate some of the water and so there will be less liquid for the pastry.)

Beat the mixture very hard with a wooden spoon or whisk until the dough forms a ball and no longer sticks to the sides of the pan and the pan is clean. Leave to cool for about 5 minutes.

Whisk the eggs in a separate bowl and then beat a small amount at a time into the pastry using a wooden spoon or a balloon whisk. The mixture will form a sticky paste which holds its shape when you lift the whisk up. When you first add the eggs and begin beating the mixture will split slightly. This is normal and the pastry will come back together as you continue to beat.

Preheat the oven to 200ºC (400ºF) Gas 6.

Spoon the choux pastry into one of the piping/pastry bags and pipe 28 thin heart shapes onto the prepared baking sheets.

Do not pipe the hearts too thickly. Pat down any peaks using a clean wet finger. Sprinkle a little water into the bottom of the oven to create steam which will help the choux to rise.

Bake in the preheated oven for 10 minutes, then reduce the oven temperature to 180ºC (350ºF) Gas 4 and bake for a further 5–10 minutes until the pastry is crisp. Remove the hearts from the oven and cut a small slit into each pastry to allow steam to escape. Leave to cool.

For the sugar glaze, mix the icing sugar with 1–2 tablespoons of water, the vanilla extract and a few drops of pink food colouring until you have a runny icing. Dip the tops of 14 hearts into the icing, invert and place on a rack. Decorate the iced hearts with sugar flowers while the icing is still wet and leave to set.

For the marshmallow filling, whisk together the icing sugar, butter, marshmallow fluff and milk until you have a smooth thick frosting. Spoon this into the remaining piping/pastry bag and pipe small blobs of filling onto the un-iced choux hearts following their shape.

To assemble, top each marshmallow filled heart with an iced and decorated top, and serve.

Mini ice cream cakes

These cold, cracking cakes are the highbrow equivalent of sobbing into a tub of ice cream, and the perfect finale to your Lovesick Tea. An appetizing, alternative fairytale ending.

FOR THE CAKE MIXTURE

225g/generous 1 cup dark brown sugar

225g/2 sticks butter, softened

4 eggs

150g/1 cup plus 2 tablespoons self-raising/self-rising flour

30 g/⅓ cup unsweetened cocoa powder

100 g/1 cup ground almonds/almond meal

2 tablespoons natural/plain yogurt

FOR THE GLAZE

100 g/3½ oz. plain/bittersweet chocolate, broken into pieces

1 tablespoon golden syrup or light corn syrup

15 g/1 tablespoon butter

100 ml/⅓ cup double/heavy cream

2 heaped tablespoons icing/confectioners' sugar, sifted

TO ASSEMBLE & DECORATE

400 ml/scant 1¾ cups vanilla ice cream

crystallized rose petals

a 35 x 25-cm/14 x 10-inch baking pan, greased and lined

a 6-cm/2½-inch round chef's ring or cookie cutter

MAKES 8 MINI CAKES

Bring the ice cream to room temperature but do not let it melt. Tip into a tray about 2-cm/1-inch deep and spread out with a spatula. Return to the freezer to set in a single layer.

Preheat the oven to 180ºC (350ºF) Gas 4.

For the cake mixture, in a mixing bowl, whisk together the brown sugar and butter until light and creamy. Add the eggs, one at a time, whisking after each egg is added. Sift in the self-raising flour and fold in with the cocoa powder. Fold in the ground almonds and the yogurt. Spoon the mixture into the prepared baking pan and bake in the preheated oven for 25–30 minutes until the cake is firm to touch and a knife comes out clean. Turn the cake out onto a wire rack and leave to cool completely.

When cool, remove the lining paper and place the cake on a chopping board. Using the chef's ring or cookie cutter, stamp out 16 circles of cake.

For the glaze, place the chocolate, syrup, butter and cream in a saucepan and simmer over a gentle heat until the chocolate and butter have melted and you have a smooth glossy sauce. Beat in the icing sugar. Pass the glaze through a fine-mesh sieve/strainer to remove any lumps of icing sugar.

Place the cakes on a wire rack to cool with a sheet of foil or parchment paper underneath to catch any drips. While the glaze is still hot, pour it over the cakes to cover. Decorate with crystallized rose petals and leave to set.

When you are ready to serve, remove the ice cream from the freezer and use the chef's ring or cookie cutter to cut out discs the same size as the cakes. Sandwich an ice cream disc between two of the glazed and decorated cakes and serve immediately, with a fork or spoon!

A PARISIAN TEA
inspired by Madame Delacroix

Formosa oolong tea

Mini croque-monsieurs

Macarons

Raspberry & lemon mille-feuilles

Strawberry sablés

Croquembouche

If you like your afternoon delights with a slice of *je ne sais quoi*, indulge in this elegant Parisian Tea, fit for the most sophisticated mademoiselle. Although the seamstress and owner of fancy dress boutique Modiste is a mistress of deception with her 'French' accent, there's no denying that her luxury ball gowns are the *crème de la crème* of haute couture. After treating yourself to some crisp mini croque-monsieurs, zingy mille-feuilles and melt-in-the-mouth macarons, you may need to ask the expert dressmaker to take you up a size. *C'est la vie!*

Formosa oolong tea

With a soft, peachy flavour, this tempting tea offers its fair share of steaming oolong-la-la!

8 teaspoons Formosa oolong tea leaves

FOR 1 POT OF TEA

Warm the teapot and add the tea leaves. Boil the kettle and allow the water to cool slightly. Pour the water over the leaves and leave to infuse for 4–10 minutes, depending on taste.

Mini croque-monsieurs

The monsieurs of Bridgerton would likely be most offended if you referred to them as 'mini'. While these tasty bites may not be comparable in size to the handsome lords, they do have other things in common: they're rich, hot and utterly delicious.

1 French-style baguette
2 teaspoons Dijon mustard
115 g/4 oz. Gruyère cheese, grated
12 slices Prosciutto or other ham
butter, at room temperature
chopped flat-leaf parsley, to garnish
salt and freshly ground black pepper, to season

MAKES 12

Cut 24 thin slices of baguette. Spread half the slices with mustard, then top with half the cheese and a piece of Prosciutto. Top with the remaining slices of bread. Preheat the grill/broiler to high. Lightly butter the sandwiches on both sides, then arrange them on a grill pan. Grill until golden, then turn over and grill until just golden on the second side. Sprinkle with the remaining cheese and grill for 1 minute, or until the cheese is bubbling. Sprinkle with parsley and grind some black pepper over them before serving.

Macarons

The elite of ton love a decadent nibble whilst discussing the intricacies of snagging a suitor. Enter the mouth-watering macaron. Ton appétit!

2 egg whites
115 g/1 heaping cup ground almonds/almond meal
115 g/1 cup icing/confectioners' sugar
storebought caramel spread, to fill

2 baking sheets, lined and greased
a disposable piping/pastry bag

MAKES ABOUT 16

Preheat the oven to 180°C (350°F) Gas 4. Put the egg whites in a clean, grease-free bowl and whisk until stiff peaks form. Combine the almonds and sugar in a separate bowl, then sift into the egg whites and fold together. Spoon mixture into a piping/pastry bag and pipe 32 2-cm/1-inch rounds on the sheets. Bake in the oven for 10 minutes. Let cool slightly, then using a palette knife transfer to a wire rack to cool. Sandwich 2 together with caramel spread to assemble.

Raspberry & lemon mille-feuilles

It's a pretty flaky person who pretends to be from a different country in order to exude an air of sophistication. This flaky, buttery French pastry surely must be a favourite of the artful Madame Delacroix.

250 g/9 oz. ready-made puff pastry dough, thawed if frozen
5 tablespoons lemon curd
300 ml/10½ fl. oz. crème fraîche/ sour cream
400 g/2½ cups fresh raspberries
icing/confectioners' sugar, to dust

a baking sheet, greased and lined

MAKES 8

Preheat the oven to 200ºC (400ºF) Gas 6.

Roll out the pastry to a thickness of 5 mm/¼, then trim it to a 30-cm x 15-cm/12 x 6 inch rectangle. Using a sharp knife, slice the pastry into 8 squares of equal size and arrange them on the baking sheet.

Bake in the preheated oven for about 10 minutes, until puffed up and golden. Transfer to a wire rack to cool.

Once cool, use a serrated knife to carefully cut each pastry square in half horizontally to create 16 pieces. When ready to assemble the mille-feuilles, arrange 8 of the pastry rectangles on a serving platter.

Fold the lemon curd into the crème fraîche and spread about 2 tablespoons of the lemon cream on top of each one. Top with raspberries and a second pastry rectangle. Dust lightly with icing sugar as soon as possible.

Strawberry sablés

When fluent-in-French Marina almost outs Genevieve for her 'unique' accent, the sly dressmaker should have had a handful of these shortbread cookies close by to shove into her mouth, making it impossible for others to notice her less-than-authentic Parisian pronunciation.

225 g/1¾ cups plain/all-purpose flour

50 g/½ cup ground almonds/ almond meal

a pinch of salt

75 g/½ cup plus ½ tablespoon icing/confectioners' sugar

130 g/½ cup plus 1 tablespoon unsalted butter, diced

1 egg plus a little extra beaten egg for glazing

½ teaspoon pure vanilla extract

225 g/1½ cups very small strawberries

icing/confectioners' sugar, for dusting

2 baking sheets, greased and lined

a 6 cm/2¼ inch cookie cutter

MAKES ABOUT 30 SABLES

Put the flour, almonds, salt and sugar in a food processor and pulse briefly to combine. Add the butter and pulse until the mixture resembles fine breadcrumbs. Beat together the egg and vanilla, then, with the machine still running, add the egg and process until the mixture just starts to come together and form a dough. Shape the dough into a ball, wrap it in clingfilm/ plastic wrap and chill in the fridge for at least 1 hour.

Preheat the oven to 180ºC (350ºF) Gas 4.

Roll out the chilled dough on a lightly floured surface to a thickness of about 5 mm/ ¼ inch, then use the cookie cutter to stamp out rounds. Re-roll any trimmings to make more rounds. Arrange the rounds on the prepared baking sheets. Prick each one a few times with the tines of a fork, and brush with a little of the beaten egg.

Bake in the preheated oven for about 15 minutes, until golden brown. Transfer to a wire rack to cool completely.

When ready to assemble, place 3 strawberries on half the cookies, then top with the remaining cookies. (Alternatively, serve the strawberries in small glass bowls with the sablés on the side.)

Dust liberally with icing sugar and serve immediately.

Croquembouche

A carefully constructed French dessert, this tower of choux-pastry puffs is almost as delicate as Madame Delacroix's web of deceit. One misplaced profiterole/mispronounced word and the whole thing could come crashing down into a sticky mess.

FOR THE CHOUX PASTRY

260 g/2 cups plain/all-purpose flour, sifted twice

200 g/1¾ sticks butter, cut into cubes

a pinch of salt

8 eggs

FOR THE FILLING

600 ml/2½ cups double/heavy cream

2 tablespoons icing/confectioners' sugar

1 teaspoon vanilla bean powder or 2 teaspoons pure vanilla extract

TO ASSEMBLE & DECORATE

600 g/2 cups caster/white granulated sugar

food-safe flowers, such as jasmine flowers

4 baking sheets, greased and lined

2 piping/pastry bags fitted with round nozzles/tips

a large sheet of thin cardboard

Sellotape/Scotch tape

SERVES 20–30

Heat the butter in a large saucepan with 600 ml/2½ cups of water and the salt until the butter is melted. As soon as the butter is melted, quickly add the sifted flour all in one go and remove the pan from the heat. Do not let the water boil for longer than it takes to melt the butter, as it will evaporate. Beat the mixture very hard with a wooden spoon until it forms a ball and no longer sticks to the sides of the pan. It is important to beat the mixture well at this stage. Let cool for 5 minutes.

In a separate bowl, whisk the eggs, then beat them into the pastry dough, a small amount at a time, using a wooden spoon or a balloon whisk. Beat the mixture very hard at each stage. The mixture will form a sticky paste that holds its shape when you lift the whisk up.

Preheat the oven to 200ºC (400ºF) Gas 6.

Spoon the choux pastry into the piping/pastry bag and pipe about 80 small balls of pastry onto the baking sheets. Using a clean, wet finger, smooth down any peaks.

Sprinkle a little water into the bottom of the oven to create steam. Bake the first baking sheet of profiteroles for about 10 minutes, then reduce the oven to 180ºC (350ºF) Gas 4 and bake for 10–15 minutes more until crisp. Cut a slit into each profiterole to allow any steam to escape, then let cool on a wire rack. Repeat with the remaining sheets. Once cool, make a small hole in the base of each profiterole using a sharp knife. For the filling, whisk together the cream, icing sugar and vanilla to stiff peaks, then spoon into the remaining piping/pastry bag. Pipe a small amount of cream into each of the profiteroles.

Make a cone with the cardboard, trimming the base so it stands flat, approximately 40 cm/16 inches high and 18 cm/7 inches in diameter across the base, securing in place with tape. Place on a stable cake stand.

In a saucepan set over a medium heat, heat the sugar until melted. Do not stir, but swirl the pan to ensure that the sugar does not burn. Once the sugar has melted, carefully dip each bun into the caramel using tongs. Place the dipped profiteroles in a ring around the base of the cone. Repeat with all the remaining profiteroles and build them up around the cone. Reheat the sugar if it becomes too solid. Once the tower is assembled, dip a fork into the remaining sugar and then spin it over the tower of profiteroles in thin lines.

Serve at once, as the spun sugar will soften over time.

A CONFIDANTE'S TEA
inspired by Lady Danbury

Ginger tea

Caramelized fennel & prawn polenta crostini

Lemon verbena semolina cookies

Lemon syllabub

Lady Grey tea cake

Make way for the all-seeing, all-knowing Lady Danbury. She will be hosting her no-nonsense afternoon tea in her opulent 'den of iniquity', where you're required to eat, drink and be married. Place your bets, while tucking into polenta crostini with shrimp, lemon syllabub, lemon verbena semolina cookies and Lady Grey tea cake. Don't even think about not attending – your regrets would certainly be denied by the candid, kick-ass confidante to the Duke of Hastings. To command the respect she deserves, Lady Danbury had to sharpen her wit, her wardrobe and her eye. You should do the same… right after you've finished eating.

Ginger tea

The straight-shooting Lady Danbury slices through all the hooey. As you're slicing through some ginger, you'll soon feel similarly formidable.

3 heaped teaspoons green tea leaves

1.5-cm/¾-inch piece fresh ginger, sliced

honey, to taste

FOR 1 POT OF TEA

Warm the teapot, add the tea leaves and ginger and pour over boiled water. Brew for 5 minutes before serving and sweeten to taste with honey.

Caramelized fennel & prawn/shrimp polenta crostini

This is quite an involved recipe so – as Lady D advises Simon – 'Do try not to bungle it up.'

grated zest of ½ a lemon and juice of 2½ lemons

2 bulbs of Florence fennel, trimmed and cut into wedges

2 teaspoons caster/white granulated sugar

50 ml/3½ tablespoons olive oil, plus extra for frying

2 garlic cloves, finely chopped

20 raw jumbo prawns/shrimp, peeled and deveined

1 tablespoon chopped fresh chives (or a few fennel fronds), to garnish

salt and freshly ground black pepper, to season

FOR THE POLENTA CROSTINI

500 ml/2 cups vegetable stock

125 g/¾ cup fine quick-cook polenta

30 g/2 tablespoons butter

50 g/⅔ cup finely grated Parmesan cheese

a baking sheet, greased and lined

a 3 cm/1 ¼ inch cookie cutter

MAKES 20

For the polenta crostini, heat the stock in a saucepan until boiling. Turn the heat down slightly and slowly add the polenta, stirring all the time. Continue to stir until the polenta is thick and smooth, and comes away from the sides of the pan. Remove from the heat and stir in the butter and Parmesan cheese. Spoon onto the prepared baking sheet and spread out to about 1 cm/½ inch deep.

Leave to set. When the polenta is completely cold, cut into circles about 3 cm/1¼ inch in diameter using a cookie cutter or the top of a small glass.

Preheat the oven to 190ºC (375ºF) Gas 5.

Fill a saucepan with water and add the juice of 1 lemon. Drop the wedges of fennel immediately into the water.

Bring the water to the boil, turn the heat down and simmer for 10 minutes. Drain the fennel and lay it in a single layer on a baking sheet. Squeeze over the juice of 1 lemon, scatter over the sugar and season. Roast for 25–30 minutes, until golden.

Meanwhile, bring a large saucepan of salted water to the boil. Mix the olive oil, garlic, lemon zest and remaining lemon juice together in a large mixing bowl and season to taste. Drop the prawns into the boiling water and cook for 2 minutes, until pink and lightly cooked. Lift them from the pan with a slotted spoon and drop them straight into the oil mixture. Stir and cool.

To assemble the crostini, brush the polenta bases with a little oil and cook on a hot griddle pan until golden. Top each with the caramelized fennel and a prawn. Garnish with chopped chives or fennel fronds and serve.

Lemon verbena semolina cookies

Verbena flowers represent protection, healing and happiness – the same things the wise Lady Danbury offered the damaged Duke growing up.

grated zest and freshly squeezed juice of 1 lemon

½ teaspoon dried lemon verbena tea leaves

200 g/1 cup caster/superfine sugar, plus extra for dipping

¼ teaspoon salt

110 g/1 stick unsalted butter, softened

1½ tablespoons extra virgin olive oil

2 eggs plus 1 egg yolk

1 tablespoon vanilla extract or ½ vanilla pod, seeds only

280 g/2 cups plain/all-purpose flour, sifted

140 g/1 cup fine semolina

1 teaspoon baking powder

¼ teaspoon bicarbonate of/ baking soda

baking sheets, greased and lined

MAKES ABOUT 20

Using an electric mixer with paddle or beater attachment (or an electric whisk), mix together the lemon zest, tea leaves, sugar and salt, and beat until the sugar smells very lemony – about 1 minute. The sugar will bruise the lemon zest and tea leaves, releasing the essential oils.

Add the butter, olive oil and lemon juice and beat until white and fluffy.

Beat the eggs and egg yolk together in a small bowl. Slowly mix into the butter mixture, beating continuously. Scrape down the batter from the side of the bowl and beat again until thoroughly combined. The mixture should look like a whipped, shiny mayonnaise. Add the vanilla extract and mix.

Mix the flour, semolina, baking powder and bicarbonate of soda together. Tip straight into the butter mixture and stir until just combined.

The dough will be very soft. Still in the bowl, press it down with clingfilm/plastic wrap to remove any big air bubbles, cover well with the clingfilm/plastic wrap and refrigerate for 1 hour.

Preheat the oven to 170ºC (340ºF) Gas 5.

Pull off pieces of dough the size of golf balls and roll into neat balls with your hands. Dip them thoroughly in caster sugar and place on the prepared baking sheets, spacing them apart to allow for spreading during baking. Slightly flatten each ball into a disc with the palm of your hand.

Bake in the preheated oven for 12 minutes. The cookies should be a light golden colour and the tops should look dry and matte.

Remove from the oven and let cool on the baking sheets for 1 minute. Transfer the cookies to a wire rack and let rest for 20 minutes or until firm to the touch.

Lemon syllabub

Lady Danbury – the juggernaut in a jaunty hat – may be sharp and acerbic but, like this dessert, she also has much sweetness running through her.

8 lemons
400 g/2 cups caster/superfine
    sugar
500 ml/2 cups double/heavy
    cream
2 teaspoons pure vanilla extract
5 strawberries

SERVES 10

Finely grate the zest from the lemons, then cut them in half and juice them. Strain out any pips and add the juice to the zest. Add the sugar to the lemon mixture. Pour half of it into a pan and heat gently to reduce to a syrup. Chill.

Whip the cream until it forms soft peaks. Fold in the remaining lemon mixture and the vanilla extract. Pour the chilled lemon syrup into the bottom of 10 flute glasses. Using a piping/pastry bag fitted with a large star nozzle/tip, pipe the syllabub into the glasses. Garnish with a slice of strawberry and refrigerate for 1 hour before serving.

Lady Grey tea cake

What sweet dish could be more fitting for Lady Danbury, whose hair is stunningly streaked with grey? As with this cake, the silver sister is unapologetically rich and fabulous.

1 Earl Grey tea bag

1 tablespoon runny honey

300 g/2 generous cups sultanas/golden raisins

80 g/generous ⅓ cup caster/white granulated sugar

2 eggs

grated zest of 1 lemon

280 g/2 generous cups self-raising/self-rising flour, sifted

1 tablespoon dried cornflower petals (optional)

icing/confectioners' sugar, for dusting

a 23-cm/9-inch square cake pan, greased and lined

SERVES 8

Begin by soaking the fruit. Pour 250 ml/1 cup boiling water over the tea bag in a bowl and leave to steep for 2–3 minutes. Remove the tea bag and add the honey and sultanas. Leave to soak for 2–3 hours until the fruit is plump. Strain the fruit, reserving the tea as this will be added to the cake batter later.

Preheat the oven to 180ºC (350ºF) Gas 4.

Whisk together the sugar and eggs until thick and creamy. Stir in the drained fruit, lemon zest, flour and petals, if using. Pour in the reserved tea, whisking all the time. Spoon the mixture into the prepared cake pan and bake for 45–60 minutes, until the cake is golden brown and a knife inserted into the centre of the cake comes out clean. Leave to cool in the pan for a few minutes, then turn out onto a wire rack to cool completely.

To serve, simply dust with icing sugar. Place a paper cake doily on top of the cake before dusting, if you want to create a pretty pattern with the sugar.

A TIPSY TEA

inspired by Lord Featherington

The Featherington martini
Crab mayonnaise éclairs
Chocolate & hazelnut biscotti
Chocolate liquor pudding
Mulled wine chocolate wreath

Archibald Featherington is a weak man with a strong desire to conceal this fact. Throughout most of *Bridgerton*, he remains steadfastly silent, reading his newspaper and lying by omission to his none-the-wiser wife. But we soon discover that, with his excessive gambling, he's gotten himself into quite the pickle. Partial to a tipple or two, his Tipsy Tea is a scandalously scrumptious spread of boozy bites, drunken delights and spirited snacks. Will it leave you satisfied, smiling and perhaps a little bit sloshed? You bet! Actually, Lord Featherington does.

The Featherington martini

The stakes are high. And so are everyone's emotions. This red cocktail represents the colour the bookies see when they realise Lord 'fraudster' Featherington has taken them for a ride.

50 ml/2 fl. oz. gin
15 ml/½ fl. oz. Italian vermouth
1 dash orange bitters
1 dash maraschino
a lemon zest twist, to garnish

Fill a cocktail shaker with ice cubes and add all the ingredients except the garnish. Stir well and strain into a chilled cocktail glass. Garnish with a lemon twist and serve immediately.

〜〜〜〜〜〜〜〜〜〜〜〜〜〜〜〜

Crab mayonnaise éclairs

The King of Bad Decisions tries desperately to hide his shady shenanigans, but it's only a matter of time before the bolshy Portia discovers that, like with these appetizing éclairs, something fishy is going on.

FOR THE ECLAIRS

75 ml/5 tablespoons full-fat/ whole milk

60 g/4 tablespoons butter

100 g/¾ cup plain/all-purpose flour

a pinch of cayenne pepper

a pinch of dry mustard powder

3 eggs, lightly beaten

1–2 tablespoons finely grated Parmesan cheese

salt and freshly ground black pepper, to season

FOR THE CRAB MAYONNAISE

4 tablespoons mayonnaise

finely grated zest and juice of ½ a lemon

½–1 teaspoon Dijon mustard

a pinch of cayenne pepper

250 g/8 oz. white crab meat

wild rocket/arugula, to serve

a large piping/pastry bag fitted with a 1-cm/⅜-inch plain nozzle/tip

2 baking sheets, greased and lined

MAKES ABOUT 30

Preheat the oven to 180ºC (350ºF) Gas 4.

Put 75 ml/5 tablespoons of water in a medium pan with the milk and butter and set over a medium heat. Stir constantly to melt the butter. As soon as the mixture comes to the boil, reduce the heat slightly and, working quickly and keeping the pan over a low heat, stir in the flour, cayenne pepper and mustard powder. Season well with salt and black pepper. Beat vigorously until the mixture is smooth and cleanly leaves the sides of the pan – this will take about 2 minutes.

Transfer the dough to a stand mixer or mixing bowl using a handheld electric whisk and gradually beat in the eggs 1 tablespoon at a time. You might not need all of the egg – when the dough is soft and smooth and drops off a spoon leaving a 'V' shape behind it is ready.

Scoop the dough into the piping/pastry bag and pipe 30 éclair buns onto the prepared baking sheets leaving plenty of space between each one. Scatter with grated Parmesan cheese and bake on the middle shelves of the preheated oven for 10–15 minutes until well risen, golden brown and sound hollow in the middle when tapped.

Remove from the oven and make a small hole in the side of each bun with a sharp knife.

Return to the oven for a further 1 minute to dry out the insides. Leave to cool on a wire rack until completely cold.

To make the crab mayonnaise, spoon the mayonnaise into a bowl, add the lemon zest and juice, mustard, cayenne pepper and a good seasoning of salt and black pepper. Mix to combine and taste. Add more salt and black pepper if required, then add the crab meat and stir gently to coat.

To assemble, use a serrated knife to split the éclairs in half, lay wild rocket leaves in the bottom of each one and top with a heaped teaspoonful of crab mayonnaise. Put the lids on and serve at once.

Chocolate & hazelnut biscotti

It's crunch time for Lord Featherington. And for you as you munch on some beautiful, twice-baked biscotti. Dunk in dessert wine for the ultimate delectation, then make like Lord F and knock the rest of the glass back.

115 g/1 scant cup plain/ all-purpose flour

1 teaspoon baking powder

a pinch of salt

80 g/⅓ cup plus 1 tablespoon caster/white granulated sugar

1 egg, beaten

100 g/⅔ cup blanched and roasted hazelnuts, roughly chopped

100 g/⅔ cup dark/bittersweet chocolate chips

1–2 baking sheets, greased and lined

MAKES ABOUT 24

Preheat the oven to 180°C (350°F) Gas 4.

Sift the flour and baking powder into a large bowl and stir in the salt and sugar.

Stir in the egg until the mixture begins to come together, then knead to form a dough. The mixture will be dry at first, but keep gently kneading until you get a smooth consistency. Add the nuts and chocolate chips and work them into the dough until evenly distributed.

Turn the dough out onto a lightly floured surface and divide into 2 pieces.

Using lightly floured hands, roll the dough into 2 sausages. Arrange the sausages on one of the prepared baking sheets, spaced well apart to allow for spreading.

Bake in the preheated oven for 25 minutes, or until the dough has risen, spread and feels firm to the touch. Take the sheet out of the oven and transfer the dough to a wire rack to cool for 5 minutes, or until cool enough to handle.

Reduce the oven temperature to 140°C (275°F) Gas 1.

Using a serrated bread knife, cut the dough into slices about 1-cm/⅜-inch thick on the diagonal, then lay them flat on the baking sheets. Bake for a further 15 minutes, turn over, then bake for a final 15 minutes, or until dry and golden. Transfer the biscotti to a wire rack to cool completely.

Delicious dunked in a glass of Vin Santo, these can be stored in an airtight container for at least a fortnight.

Chocolate liquor pudding

Like the chocolate liqueurs buried in each pud, Lord Featherington tries to keep his sorry secrets hidden, too. Alas, when the heat is on, they all come spilling out, much like the oozy, boozy chocolate.

100 g/6½ tablespoons unsalted butter, softened

100 g/3½ oz. dark/bittersweet chocolate, roughly chopped

2 eggs, plus 2 egg yolks

80 g/⅓ cup plus 1 tablespoon caster/white granulated sugar

100 g/¾ cup plain/all-purpose flour

20 g/3 tablespoons unsweetened cocoa powder

6 liqueur-filled chocolates

6 ramekin dishes, greased

SERVES 6

Preheat the oven to 190ºC (375ºF) Gas 5.

Very gently, melt the butter and chocolate in the microwave on short, low bursts or alternatively in a heatproof bowl set over a pan of barely simmering water.

In a large mixing bowl, whisk the eggs, egg yolks and sugar together until light and frothy, then gently fold in the melted chocolate and butter. Sift the flour and cocoa powder over the mixture and gently fold together.

Divide the batter equally between the ramekins. Gently push a liqueur-filled chocolate into each ramekin and ensure that they are fully covered by the batter. Set the ramekins on a baking sheet and bake in the preheated oven for about 10–12 minutes.

Take the dishes out of the oven – be careful as the ramekins will be hot. Slide a sharp knife around the edge of each ramekin, then gently turn out each sponge onto a small plate to serve.

Mulled wine chocolate wreath

Perhaps the perfect cake to serve at the wake of the doomed patriarch of the Featherington family, this port-laced Bundt would, ironically, be sweetly sobering.

375 ml/1⅔ cups port

3 eggs

350 ml/1½ cups milk

185 g/1½ sticks butter, melted and cooled

400 g/2 cups caster/white granulated sugar

grated zest and juice of 1 orange

1 teaspoon vanilla paste

a pinch of salt

335 g/2⅔ cups plain/all-purpose flour

125 g/1 cup cocoa powder

2 teaspoons baking powder

2 teaspoons bicarbonate of/ baking soda

¼ teaspoon ground cloves

1 tablespoon ground cinnamon

¼ teaspoon ground nutmeg

winter fruits, to decorate

FOR THE GLAZE

75 g/2½ oz. dark/bittersweet chocolate, broken into pieces

75 g/5 tablespoons butter, cut into cubes

1 tablespoon golden/light corn syrup

50 ml/3 tablespoons port

a 25-cm/10-inch cake ring/Bundt pan, greased and floured

SERVES 8

Preheat the oven to 180ºC (350ºF) Gas 4.

Heat the port in a saucepan set over a gentle heat until just boiling. In the meantime, whisk together the eggs, milk and melted butter in a large mixing bowl. Mix in the sugar, orange zest and juice, vanilla and salt. Sift in the flour, cocoa and raising agents and add the spices before whisking until thoroughly combined. Continue to whisk while gradually adding the hot port. The batter will be very wet.

Pour the mixture into the prepared cake pan and bake in the preheated oven for about 40–45 minutes, or until an inserted skewer comes out clean. Leave the cake to cool in its pan on top of a wire rack for 10 minutes, before turning out and to cool completely.

Put all of the glaze ingredients into a small pan set over a gentle heat and stir until the chocolate and butter have melted and the glaze is streak free. Leave to cool until thick enough to pour without it rolling off the sides of the cake.

Place a sheet of parchment paper underneath the wire rack to catch any drips. Pour the glaze over the cold cake. Decorate with winter fruits and leave the cake to set completely at room temperature before transferring to a serving plate or cake stand.

A FLORAL TEA
inspired by Lady Featherington

Jasmine flowering tea

Rosemary scones with cream cheese & Parma ham

Lavender shortbread

Dark chocolate floral cake

Meringues with rosewater cream

White chocolate & rose cookies

Lady Portia Featherington is anything but a shrinking violet. She's scheming, manipulative and wants nothing more than to find suitable husbands for her daughters (whilst keeping the scandals hush-hush). Never opting for an understated look, her floral frocks are nothing short of splendid – if not a tad gaudy. Sitting down to this spread, she'll blend right in (watch out for bees, Portia!) as she tucks into scones, shortbread and rosewater-cream meringues. Her life may be complicated, but at least whilst she's enjoying her tea, everything seems like it's coming up roses.

Jasmine flowering tea

This delicate, sweet tea is said to aid weight loss and combat bad breath. In Lady Featherington's plight to marry her daughters off, it's a wonder she's not forcing them to mainline the stuff!

1 jasmine flowering tea ball

FOR 1 POT OF TEA

Warm a teapot (glass if you have one). Add the tea ball and pour in very slightly cooled boiled water. In 2–3 minutes the bundle will have unfurled and the tea will be ready to drink. Refill the pot up to 3 times.

Rosemary scones with cream cheese & Parma ham

Portia does her darndest to conceal the scandal going on in her household. But, like with these lip-smacking savoury scones, one bite (observant member of the ton) and the secrets (cream cheese) will come oozing out the sides.

225 g/1¾ cups plus 1 tablespoon self-raising/self-rising flour

1 teaspoon baking powder

¼ teaspoon salt

2 teaspoons chopped fresh rosemary needles

50 g/3½ tablespoons butter

100 ml/3½ fl. oz. full-fat/whole milk

1 egg

150 g/5½ oz. cream cheese

85 g/3 oz. thinly sliced Parma ham or other ham

100 g/⅔ cup seedless grapes, halved

a 4–5-cm/2-inch diameter cookie cutter

a baking sheet, greased and lined

MAKES 12

Preheat the oven to 220ºC (425ºF) Gas 7.

Put the flour, baking powder, salt and rosemary in a food processor and pulse to combine. Add the butter and process for about 20 seconds until the mixture resembles fine breadcrumbs.

Tip into a large bowl and make a well in the middle. Beat together the egg and milk, then reserve 1 tablespoon of the mixture. Pour the remaining mixture into the flour and work it in using a fork. Turn out on to a floured surface and knead briefly to make a soft, smooth dough. Roll or pat out the dough to a thickness of about 2.5 cm/1 inch and stamp out 12 rounds with the cookie cutter. Arrange them on the prepared baking sheet, spacing them slightly apart, and brush with the reserved egg and milk mixture.

Bake in the preheated oven for about 8 minutes until risen and golden, then transfer to a wire rack to cool.

Serve spread with cream cheese and topped with Parma ham and halved grapes.

Lavender shortbread

Purple is the colour of nobility, power, luxury, grandeur and ambition. What sweet treat could be more apt for this zealous status seeker?

50 g/¼ cup caster/superfine sugar, plus extrafor sprinkling

⅓ teaspoon dried lavender flowers

175 g/1½ cups plain/all-purpose flour

115 g/1 stick unsalted butter, chilled and diced

an 18-cm/7-inch square cake pan, greased and lined

MAKES 18

Preheat the oven to 160°C (325°F) Gas 3.

Put the sugar and dried lavender flowers in a food processor and pulse briefly until the flowers are just chopped. Set aside.

Put the flour and butter in a bowl and work together with your fingertips until the mixture resembles fine breadcrumbs. Add the lavender and sugar mixture and stir to combine, then use your hands to work the mixture into a dough.

Press the dough into the base of the prepared pan, pressing it flat using the base of a glass. Prick the surface all over using the tines of a fork, then use a sharp knife to score into 18 fingers.

Sprinkle the shortbread lightly with sugar, then bake in the preheated oven for about 35–40 minutes, until a pale straw colour.

Cut into fingers along the scored lines and let cool in the pan before serving.

Dark chocolate floral cake

From her husband's mounting debts to the 'state' of her distant relative Marina staying under her roof – not to mention her daughters' inability to snag suitors – Lady Featherington perhaps needs to seek solace in this rich, forget-all-your-troubles pick-me-up.

100 g/3½ oz. plain/bittersweet chocolate

125 g/1 stick plus 1 tablespoon butter, at room temperature

170 g/¾ cup plus ½ a tablespoon caster/white granulated sugar

2 eggs, separated

170 g/1¼ cups self-raising/self-rising flour

1 tablespoon unsweetened cocoa powder

60 ml/4 tablespoons full-fat/whole milk

FOR THE FROSTING & TO DECORATE

200 g/1½ cups plain/bittersweet chocolate, chopped

200 ml/6¾ fl. oz. double/heavy cream

crystallized/candied violets

a 20-cm/8-inch springform cake pan, greased and base-lined

SERVES 8–12

Preheat the oven to 180°C (350°F) Gas 4.

Put the chocolate in a heatproof bowl and set it over a pan of barely simmering water. Let melt, stirring occasionally, then set aside to cool for about 5 minutes.

Put the butter and sugar in a large bowl and beat to combine, then beat in the egg yolks.

Fold in the melted chocolate, then sift in the flour and cocoa powder and mix to combine. Stir in the milk, a little at a time, to loosen the mixture.

In a clean, grease-free bowl, whisk the egg whites until stiff, then fold into the chocolate mixture, about a quarter at a time. Spoon the cake mixture into the prepared pan and bake in the preheated oven for about 45 minutes, until a skewer inserted in the centre comes out clean. Remove from the oven and turn out onto a wire rack to cool completely.

To decorate, put the chocolate in a heatproof bowl, then put the cream in a saucepan and heat until almost boiling.

Pour the hot cream over the chocolate and stir until melted. Leave to cool and thicken for about 10–15 minutes, then spread over the cake, smoothing it over the top and sides with a palette knife. Sprinkle with crystallized violets and let the frosting set before serving.

Meringues with rosewater cream

Like these airy bites, there are two sides to Portia Featherington. The together, 'everything's-fine' side she displays to society and the terrified 'what-to-do' side she reserves for behind closed doors.

2 egg whites

115 g/½ cup minus ¼ teaspoon caster/superfine sugar

FOR THE FILLING & TO DECORATE

200 ml/6¾ fl. oz. double/heavy cream

1½ tablespoons rosewater

a small handful of clean, fresh rose petals, to decorate (optional)

2 baking sheets, greased and lined

MAKES 8

Preheat the oven to 130ºC (250ºF) Gas ½.

Put the egg whites in a clean, grease-free bowl and whisk until they form stiff peaks. Whisk in the sugar, 1 tablespoonful at a time, until the mixture is thick and glossy. Using 2 dessert spoons, shape about 16 meringues and place them on the baking sheets.

Bake for about 2 hours, until crisp and dry. Leave to cool on the baking sheets, then carefully peel off the parchment paper.

To serve, whip the cream until it stands in soft peaks, then fold in the rosewater. Sandwich the meringues together with the cream and arrange on a serving plate. Scatter the rose petals, if using, over the meringues to decorate, and serve.

White chocolate & rose cookies

The white (as opposed to milk or dark) chocolate chips must be a blessing for the neurotic matriarch... If she got brown, chocolate smudges on one of her swanky dresses, it might just tip her over the edge...

125 g/9 tablespoons butter, at room temperature and cubed

90 g/½ cup caster/white granulated sugar

35 g/3 tablespoons muscovado/light brown sugar

1 teaspoon pure vanilla extract

2 drops of rose extract (or a few drops of rosewater)

2 teaspoons single/light cream

1 egg

200 g/1½ cups plain/all-purpose flour

½ teaspoon baking powder

½ teaspoon salt

90 g/½ cup white chocolate chips

15 g/½ oz. crystallized/candied rose petals, finely chopped

1 teaspoon crushed freeze-dried strawberries (optional)

1–2 baking sheets, greased and lined

MAKES ABOUT 25

Put the butter in a bowl and beat with a wooden spoon until very soft. Beat in the sugars until well incorporated and creamy, then add the vanilla extract, rose extract or rose water, cream and egg and beat in. Gradually sift in the flour, baking powder and salt and mix until combined. Finally, mix in the chocolate chips, rose petals and freeze-dried strawberries, if using. Cover and refrigerate for 30 minutes.

Preheat the oven to 170ºC (325ºF) Gas 3.

Remove the bowl from the fridge. Lightly flour a clean work surface and roll the chilled dough out into a sausage roughly 30 cm/12 inches long. Cut the dough into 25 equal slices and arrange on the prepared baking sheets.

Bake in the preheated oven for 15–20 minutes until golden. Allow the cookies to cool on the baking sheets for 5 minutes, then transfer to a wire rack.

A FEMINIST TEA

inspired by Eloise Bridgerton

Tippy green tea

Finger sandwiches

Garden cupcakes

Rose & raspberry choux rings

Whip-smart, opinionated and brazen, don't expect the fifth eldest of the Bridgerton clan to prepare or serve any of the treats in her Feminist Tea. She'll happily eat all the sandwiches, cupcakes and pastries on the menu – declaring 'I do not share my food' – but she will not bow to society's expectation of her to become a homemaker. Hungry for knowledge, she can't stand frivolity and believes she is destined for something much greater than marriage and baby-making. It may be a man's world but, by golly, she'll fight the women's corner with witty, astute remarks until progress is made. Bite on, sister!

Tippy green tea

With more tips (leaf buds) and caffeine than a 'non-tippy' tea, this bold, gutsy brew will leave Eloise fired up and ready to take on the ton.

4 teaspoons tippy green tea leaves

FOR 1 POT OF TEA

Warm the teapot and add the tea. Pour in boiling water and leave to brew for 4–5 minutes or so. Pour into tea glasses and serve.

~~~~~~

Finger sandwiches

Make like the ahead-of-her-time, would-be suffragette by rolling your eyes and wagging your finger (sandwiches) at the absurdity of the 'season'.

8 slices of white or wholemeal bread

butter, at room temperature, for spreading

salt and freshly ground black pepper, to season

FOR THE EGG MAYONNAISE & WATERCRESS FILLING

2 tablespoons mayonnaise

½ teaspoon Dijon mustard

2 hard-boiled/cooked eggs, cooled

a handful of watercress

FOR THE BRIE & CRANBERRY FILLING

115 g/4 oz. Brie or Camembert, at room temperature

1–1½ tablespoons cranberry jelly

MAKES 12 FINGER SANDWICHES

To make the egg mayonnaise sandwiches, thinly butter 4 slices of bread. Put the mayonnaise and mustard in a small bowl and stir to combine. Peel the eggs, put them in a separate bowl and mash well with a fork. Add the mayonnaise to the eggs and mash again until the whites have broken up and the mixture is creamy. Season to taste with salt and pepper. Divide this mixture between 2 slices of the buttered bread and spread evenly. Top each with watercress and a slice of buttered bread. To cut, put your hand on top of the sandwich and press down gently. Using a serrated knife and a gentle sawing motion, cut off the crusts. Cut each sandwich lengthways into 3 to make 6 finger sandwiches.

To make the Brie and cranberry sandwiches, thinly butter 4 slices of bread. Spread 2 slices of the buttered bread with cranberry jelly. Cut the Brie into thin slices and arrange them on top of the cranberry jelly. Season to taste with salt and pepper and top each one with a slice of the buttered bread. Using a serrated knife and a gentle sawing motion, cut off the crusts. Cut the sandwiches lengthways into 3 to make 6 finger sandwiches.

Arrange the finger sandwiches on a serving plate and cover with clingfilm/plastic wrap until ready to serve.

Garden cupcakes

Busted by her brother Benedict whilst smoking a cigarette on a swing in the garden, Eloise soon starts to confide in him. The only thing missing from this touching scene of sibling solidarity is one of these cupcakes in her other hand.

FOR THE CUPCAKE MIXTURE

½ **vanilla pod/bean**

3 **eggs**

150 g/1 cup **icing/confectioners' sugar**

150 g/1 cup plus 2 tablespoons **plain/all-purpose flour**

1 teaspoon **baking powder**

150 g/1 stick plus 3 tablespoons **butter, melted**

grated zest of ½ a lemon

wild strawberries, or chopped strawberries, and freshly chopped basil, to decorate

FOR THE LEMON BASIL CREAM

220 g/¾ cup **lemon marmalade or preserve**

5 fresh **basil leaves**

250 g/9 oz. **mascarpone**

a cupcake pan, lined with 12 cupcake cases

a piping/pastry bag, fitted with a star-shaped nozzle/tip

MAKES 12

Make the vanilla cupcake mixture the day before you want to make the cupcakes. Split the vanilla pod lengthways and scrape the seeds out into a bowl. Add the eggs and sugar and beat with an electric whisk until tripled in volume and the beaters leave a thick ribbon trail when you lift them out of the mixture. Sift the flour and baking powder into the bowl and whisk lightly. Add the melted butter and fold in gently with a large metal spoon. Fold in the lemon zest. Cover and refrigerate for 24 hours.

The next day, preheat the oven to 160ºC (325ºF) Gas 3.

Divide the mixture between the cupcake cases and bake in the preheated oven for about 15–20 minutes. Remove from the oven and allow to cool completely.

To make the lemon basil cream, put the lemon marmalade and basil leaves in a food processor and blitz until smooth. Fold this gently into the mascarpone cheese until evenly mixed.

Fill the piping/pastry bag with the lemon basil cream and pipe on top of the cold cupcakes. Decorate with wild or chopped strawberries and chopped basil.

Rose & raspberry choux rings

Eloise isn't after a ring, but if she was served one of these fruity, creamy circles of pastry perfection, she might just make an exception.

1 quantity Choux Pastry (see page 59)

FOR THE ICING & DECORATION

150 g/1¼ cups fondant icing/ confectioners' sugar, sifted
1 tablespoon rose syrup
pink food colouring
crystallized rose petals

FOR THE FILLING

300 ml/1¼ cups double/heavy cream
1 tablespoon rose syrup
280 g/2 cups fresh raspberries

a large baking sheet, greased and lined
2 piping/pastry bags, 1 fitted with a round and 1 with a star nozzle/tip
10 cupcake cases (optional)

MAKES 10

Preheat the oven to 200ºC (400ºF) Gas 6. Spoon the choux pastry into the piping/pastry bag fitted with a round nozzle/tip and pipe 10 rings of pastry, about 6 cm/2½ inch in diameter onto the baking sheet, a small distance apart. Pat down any peaks in the pastry using a clean wet finger. Sprinkle a little water into the bottom of the oven to create steam which will help the choux pastry to rise.

Bake in the preheated oven for 10 minutes, then reduce the oven temperature to 180ºC (350ºF) Gas 4 and bake for a further 15–20 minutes until the pastry is crisp. Remove from the oven and cut a small slit into each ring to allow any steam to escape and leave to cool. Carefully cut each ring in half horizontally using a sharp knife.

For the icing, mix the icing sugar with the rose syrup and a few drops of food colouring until you have a thick icing, adding a little water if needed.

Spread a little icing over the tops of the choux rings. Decorate each top with some crystallized rose petals and then leave the icing to set. Once the icing is set, whip the cream and rose syrup for the filling to stiff peaks then spoon into the piping/pastry bag fitted with a star nozzle/tip. Pipe swirls of cream into the bottom of each ring. Top with fresh raspberries then place an iced ring on top of each one. Serve straight away or store in the fridge if you are not eating straight away. These choux buns are best eaten on the day they are made.

A PUNCHY TEA
inspired by *Will Mondrich*

Tropical tea punch

Fresh spinach & herb frittata

Topped cornbread toasts

Chocolate pecan cookies

Espresso brownies

Angel food cake

Whilst many people in *Bridgerton* are fighting for a (wedding) ring, the strapping Will is fighting in the (boxing) ring. A loyal friend – and sparring partner – to Simon, the sportsman is hungry for victory... at least, until he and Lord Featherington have a little chat. Now you'll be hungry for Mr Mondrich's Punchy Tea, a knockout feast of spinach frittatas, cornbread toasts, espresso brownies, and plenty more fare that really packs a punch. Make like Daphne in the crowd at one of Will's matches and shout, 'Go on... Plant a facer!', then get ready to 'stuff your facer'.

Tropical tea punch

After going a few rounds in the ring, Will would welcome a slug or two of this sweet, chilled refreshment. He'd better not have too much though, or he'll end up punch-drunk.

3 teaspoons black tea leaves, such as Keemun or Nilgiri
1–2 tablespoons light brown sugar, to taste
600 ml/21 fl. oz. unsweetened pineapple juice, well-chilled
4 tablespoons white rum
1 lime, sliced
1 orange, sliced
1 star fruit, thinly sliced
ice cubes, to serve

SERVES 4–6

Pour a little hot water into a large teapot and leave to warm for a minute or two. Drain, add the tea leaves and pour in 600ml/2½ cups freshly boiled water. Leave the tea to brew for about 3 minutes.

Strain the tea into a large glass jug/pitcher and add sugar to taste. When it has cooled, add the pineapple juice and rum. Chill in the fridge.

To serve, add the fruit slices and plenty of ice to the jug/pitcher and pour into tumblers.

Fresh spinach & herb frittata

Eggs plus spinach equal super-strength. Will needs to tuck into this lean, green dish in order to maintain his status as a lean, mean fighting machine (*removes mouthguard*).

a handful of fresh spinach leaves
4–5 tablespoons olive oil
1 small onion, finely chopped
6 eggs, beaten
a handful of mixed fresh herbs (such as flat-leaf parsley, basil and chives), finely chopped
salt and freshly ground black pepper, to season

MAKES 3 MINI FRITTATAS

Wash the spinach thoroughly and squeeze lightly to remove excess water. Cook the spinach in a small saucepan set over a medium heat until it is wilted (this should take 2–3 minutes).

Set aside to cool, and then chop well.

Heat 2 tablespoons of the oil in a small frying pan/skillet and cook the onion until it is soft but still translucent. Leave it to cool a little and then add it to the spinach and mix well. Add the beaten eggs and mix well. Season to taste with salt and pepper, then stir in the herbs.

Add a little of the remaining oil to a very small omelette pan/skillet, set over a medium heat and pour in one-third of the mixture. Using a non-stick spoon or spatula, draw the egg mixture from the sides of the pan into the middle, until the whole frittata begins to set. Turn the heat down to low and let the frittata continue to cook until completely set.

When fully set, remove the pan/skillet from the heat and keep warm. Repeat with the remaining mixture. If preferred, you could preheat the oven to 180ºC (350ºF) Gas 4 and divide the mixture between 3 small saucer-size cake pans, and cook for about 20 minutes, until set. Or alternatively pour the whole lot into a roasting pan and cook for about 30 minutes.

Cut into slices or squares and serve warm.

Topped cornbread toasts

Vastly preferable to a knuckle sandwich, these heavyweight zesty zingers are similar to most of Will's challengers in the boxing ring; toast.

500 g/18 oz. cornbread

FOR THE CRAB SALAD TOPPING

170 g/¾ cup canned white crabmeat

½ green (bell) pepper, deseeded and diced

1 teaspoon lemon juice

2 teaspoons olive oil

a good splash of Tabasco sauce

½ garlic clove, finely chopped

1 teaspoon snipped chives

FOR THE AVOCADO SALSA TOPPING

1 ripe avocado, stoned, peeled and finely diced

2 tomatoes, deseeded and finely diced

2 spring onions/scallions, sliced

1 red chilli/chile, deseeded and finely chopped

a handful fresh coriander/ cilantro, chopped

juice of ½ a lime

salt and freshly ground black pepper, to season

MAKES 24

To make the crab salad topping, put the crabmeat and green pepper in a bowl. Put the lemon juice, olive oil, Tabasco and garlic in a small bowl and whisk to combine. Pour it over the crab and pepper mixture. Sprinkle with chives and toss well to combine. Cover and set aside.

To make the avocado salsa topping, put the avocado, tomato, spring onion and chili in a bowl.

Sprinkle with the coriander and add a pinch of salt, if liked, then squeeze the lime juice over it and toss gently to combine. Cover and set aside.

Preheat the grill/broiler. Slice the cornbread into 24 squares measuring about 5 cm x 5 cm/ 2 inch x 2 inch and 1 cm/½ inch thick. Arrange the slices under the hot grill/broiler and toast on both sides until golden brown and crisp.

To assemble, put spoonfuls of crab salad topping on to half of the toasts and avocado salsa topping on the remainder. Serve them immediately, as the toasts will lose their crispness if left too long before eating.

Chocolate pecan cookies

When the fighter is offered a path to financial freedom, he bites the bullet. He should have bitten one of these nutty numbers instead.

175 g/1½ sticks butter, at room temperature

100 g/½ cup caster/white granulated sugar

1 tablespoon full-fat/whole milk

200 g/1½ cups self-raising/self-rising flour

100 g/3½ oz. dark/bittersweet chocolate, roughly chopped

50 g/½ cup pecan nuts, roughly chopped plus extra to decorate

2–3 baking sheets, greased and lined

MAKES ABOUT 14

Preheat the oven to 180ºC (350ºF) Gas 4.

Put the butter and sugar in a bowl and beat together until smooth and creamy, then beat in the milk. Add the flour and mix to make a soft dough, then add the chocolate and pecan nuts.

Drop 14 rounded tablespoonfuls of the mixture on to the baking sheets (spacing them well apart to allow the mixture to spread), and flatten them slightly with the back of the spoon. Press a pecan half into the centre of each one.

Bake for about 15 minutes, until golden around the edges, then leave to cool on the sheets for about 5 minutes before transferring to a wire rack to cool completely.

These cookies are best eaten on the day they are baked, but will keep for a few days in an airtight container.

Espresso brownies

These coffee-laden brownies are a real hit, and would help to keep Will alert and at the top of his game. Pow!

230 g/8 oz. dark/bittersweet chocolate, chopped

115 g/1 stick butter, softened

300 g/1½ cups caster/white granulated sugar

5 eggs, lightly beaten

4 tablespoons freshly brewed strong espresso coffee, at room temperature

70 g/½ cup plain/all-purpose flour

70 g/¾ cup unsweetened cocoa powder, plus a little extra for dusting

single/light cream, to serve (optional)

a 23-cm/9-inch square baking pan, greased and lined

MAKES 20

Preheat the oven to 180ºC (350ºF) Gas 4.

Melt the chocolate in a heatproof bowl set over a pan of barely simmering water. Do not let the base of the bowl touch the water. Stir occasionally until smooth. Remove the bowl from the pan and set aside until needed.

Put the soft butter and sugar in a mixing bowl and use a wooden spoon or a hand-held electric mixer to beat until light and fluffy. Gradually beat in the eggs, then the coffee.

Sift the flour and cocoa into the bowl and stir in. Add the melted chocolate and mix in. When thoroughly combined transfer the mixture to the prepared pan, spread evenly and level the surface. Bake in the preheated oven for about 25 minutes until a skewer inserted in the middle comes out just clean. Remove the pan from the oven. Leave to cool in the pan for 10 minutes.

To serve, lightly dust with cocoa powder, remove from the pan and cut into 20 pieces. Serve warm or at room temperature with cream, if liked. Once cool, store in an airtight container and eat within 5 days.

Angel food cake

Although Will struggled with the decision of throwing a match, he ultimately listened to the devil on his shoulder. Perhaps he needed a guardian angel (or a slice of this light, ethereal cake) to steer him in the right direction.

125 g/1 cup minus 1 tablespoon plain/all-purpose flour

250 g/1¼ cups caster/white granulated sugar

10 egg whites

1 teaspoon cream of tartar

½ teaspoon pure vanilla extract

a punnet/1 cup of blueberries or 6 ripe peaches, to serve (optional)

FOR THE FROSTING

115 g/½ cup plus ¼ tablespoon caster/superfine sugar

2 egg whites

2 teaspoons golden/light corn syrup

½ teaspoon pure vanilla extract

a sugar thermometer

a 25-cm/10-inch diameter non-stick ring cake pan, lightly greased

SERVES 8–12

Preheat the oven to 180ºC (350ºF) Gas 4.

In a large bowl, sift together the flour and half the sugar 3 times, until very light. Set aside.

In a separate, grease-free bowl, whisk the egg whites with the cream of tartar until stiff, then gradually whisk in the remaining sugar until the mixture is thick and glossy. Whisk in the vanilla extract. Sift half the flour and sugar mixture into the egg whites and gently fold in, then sift in the remaining flour and fold in.

Spoon the cake mixture into the prepared mould and bake for about 40 minutes, until a skewer inserted into the cake comes out clean. Turn the cake out on to a wire rack and leave to cool completely before frosting.

To make the frosting, put the sugar in a small saucepan with 4 tablespoons water and heat, stirring until the sugar dissolves, then boil until the temperature reaches 115ºC/240ºF.

In a clean, grease-free bowl, whisk the egg whites until very stiff, then gradually pour the sugar syrup into the egg whites in a thin stream, whisking constantly until thick and glossy. Whisk in the golden syrup and vanilla extract and continue whisking until the frosting has cooled. Use a palette knife to spread it over the cooled cake.

Serve with blueberries or slices of fresh peach, as preferred.

A REBELLIOUS TEA
inspired by Marina Thompson

Rooibos red tea

Creamy tomato & mascarpone tartlets with chargrilled artichokes

Fruit buns

Lemon & lavender cakes

Strong, opinionated and… eating for two, Marina finds herself on an extremely sticky wicket. With her virtue 'compromised', the clock is ticking for her to find a gentleman dim/eager enough to marry her before he discovers her predicament. But she's no meek damsel who'll agree to marrying any old fool (sorry, Lord Rutledge); she'll fight tooth and nail with Lady Featherington in a bid to find a suitable suitor. All that dishonesty, disobedience and deceit calls for this Rebellious Tea, which will keep Marina's strength – and spirits – up. Defiantly delectable.

Rooibos red tea

By far more palatable – and less dangerous – than the herbal concoction Marina prepares herself to 'sort things out', this earthy, nutty tea will offer comfort in turbulent times.

3 teaspoons rooibos tea leaves or use equivalent in tea bags

sugar, lemon or honey, to taste

FOR 1 POT OF TEA

Warm the teapot and add the tea. Pour over boiling water. Stir gently and leave to infuse for 3–4 minutes. Sweeten to taste, but always serve without milk.

~~~~~~

Creamy tomato & mascarpone tartlets with chargrilled artichokes

Once Marina accepts that she's going to be a mother, she might want to start looking after herself and her unborn child. Artichokes are a pregnancy power food, so these teeny tarts would be an excellent place to start.

FOR THE PASTRY

85 g/1 cup minus ¾ tablespoon plain/all-purpose flour

40 g/3 tablespoons butter, chilled and diced

40 g/½ cup finely grated Parmesan cheese

FOR THE FILLING

1½ tablespoons olive oil

1 garlic clove, finely chopped

1 large red (bell) pepper, deseeded and chopped

1½ tablespoons mascarpone

½ teaspoon cider vinegar

½ handful fresh basil leaves, chopped, plus extra to garnish

2 marinated artichoke hearts, drained

salt and freshly ground black pepper, to season

a 6.5 cm/2.5 inch diameter cookie cutter

a 12-cup mini tartlet pan, greased

MAKES 12

To make the pastry, put the flour, butter and Parmesan cheese in a food processor and process until the mixture resembles fine breadcrumbs.

Gradually add 1 tablespoon iced water until the mixture comes together. Shape into a ball, wrap in clingfilm/plastic wrap and chill for 1 hour.

To make the filling, gently fry the garlic and (bell) pepper in the oil over low heat for 15 minutes until soft, then tip into a food processor and blend until smooth.

Transfer the mixture to a bowl, and stir in the mascarpone cheese, vinegar and chopped basil. Season to taste, cover and set aside.

Preheat the oven to 190ºC (350ºF) Gas 5.

Roll out the pastry on a lightly floured surface and stamp out 12 rounds using the cookie cutter. Press the rounds into the tartlet pan and prick the base of each with a fork.

Bake in the preheated oven for about 12 minutes, until crisp and golden. Transfer to a wire rack to cool.

To serve, cut each artichoke heart into 6 wedges. Spoon a little red pepper mixture into each tartlet case, top with artichoke and grind a little black pepper on top to serve.

Fruit buns

So there's a bun in the oven...
and many more on the table!

500 g/4 cups plain/all-purpose
    white flour

2.5 g/1¼ teaspoons instant yeast,
    5 g/1¾ teaspoons dry yeast, or
    10 g/2 teaspoons fresh yeast

150 g/¾ cup caster/white
    granulated sugar

250 g/1 cup milk, heated then
    cooled to room temperature

10 g/2½ teaspoons salt

1 egg

finely grated zest of 1 large lemon

100 g/6½ tablespoons butter,
    melted and cooled

100 g/⅔ cup dark raisins, soaked
    in water or the alcohol of your
    choice overnight, or while your
    dough is resting if you have
    forgotten to soak them the
    night before

FOR THE GLAZE

1 egg

1 tablespoon water

a pinch of salt

a pinch of sugar

2 baking sheets, greased and lined

MAKES 12 BUNS

Put the flour into a large mixing bowl and make a well. Sprinkle the yeast and sugar into the well and pour over the milk. Flick some flour over the milk to close the well and then cover with a tea towel/dish cloth.

Allow to rest for 1 hour. Add the salt, egg, lemon zest and melted butter and bring the ingredients together in the bowl. Turn the dough out on the counter and knead it well for 10 minutes. Put it back in the bowl, cover and allow to rest for 30 minutes.

Drain the soaked raisins and dump them on top of the dough in the bowl. Work them in gently so you don't squash them. Once the raisins are worked in, cover the bowl again and allow the dough to rest for 2 hours. Pull the dough gently out onto an unfloured surface.

Divide the dough into 12 equal portions. Shape each portion into a tight ball and place them on a prepared baking sheet. Cover with a dry tea/kitchen towel and allow to rest for 45 minutes.

Preheat the oven to 220ºC (425ºF) Gas 7.

Beat together the ingredients for the glaze and generously brush the tops of the buns with the glaze before popping them into the preheated oven for 15 minutes. They should sound hollow when they are done. Remove from the oven and cool completely on a wire rack. To serve, split and spread with the butter.

Lemon & lavender cakes

Life may have given her lemons, but the Featherington's distant cousin could add lavender, sugar and food colouring to make this lovely layered cake. Everything looks brighter when you have something mauve to munch on!

FOR THE LAVENDER FLOWERS

10 sprigs of edible lavender
1 egg white
caster/superfine sugar,
    for sprinkling

FOR THE CAKE MIXTURE

340 g/3 sticks butter, softened
340 g/1¾ cups caster/white
    granulated sugar
6 eggs
340 g/2½ cups self-raising/
    self-rising flour, sifted
3 teaspoons baking powder
3 tablespoons buttermilk or
    sour cream

grated zest of 3 lemons
purple food colouring gel
icing/confectioners' sugar,
    for dusting

**FOR THE DRIZZLE & LAVENDER
LEMON CURD**

freshly squeezed juice of
    5 lemons
1 teaspoon edible lavender
2 tablespoons icing/
    confectioners' sugar
3 tablespoons lemon curd

FOR THE BUTTERCREAM

350 g/2½ cups icing
    confectioners' sugar, sifted
1 tablespoon cream cheese
15 g/1 tablespoon butter,
    softened
freshly squeezed juice of 1 lemon

a paintbrush
a baking sheet, greased and lined
three 20-cm/8-inch round cake
    pans, greased and lined
a 6.5-cm/2½-inch cookie cutter
a piping/pastry bag fitted with
    small round nozzle/tip

MAKES 10

Begin by preparing the lavender flowers, as they will need to dry overnight.

Whisk the egg white until very foamy. Using a paintbrush, brush the flower sprigs with egg white, then sprinkle with sugar. Repeat with all the flowers, one at a time, and place on the prepared baking sheet.

Leave in a warm place to dry overnight. Once dried, store in an airtight container until needed.

To make the cake mixture, use an electric whisk to mix the butter and sugar in a bowl until light and creamy. Add the eggs and whisk again. Fold in the flour, baking powder and buttermilk or sour cream using a spatula, until incorporated.

Preheat the oven to 180°C (350°F) Gas 4.

Fold the lemon zest into the cake mixture. Spoon one-third of the mixture into one of the prepared cake pans. Add a few drops of food colouring to the cake mixture and whisk in so that you have an even pale purple colour. Spoon half of the coloured mixture into another of the cake pans. Add a few more drops of food colouring to the remaining batter to make it a darker purple colour, then spoon the mixture into the final pan. Bake in the preheated oven for 25–30 minutes, until they are firm to

the touch and a knife inserted into the centre of each cake comes out clean.

To make the drizzle, set a small saucepan over a medium heat, heat the lemon juice, lavender and icing sugar and bring to the boil. Mix one tablespoon of this syrup with the lemon curd and set aside, then spoon the remaining syrup over the cakes and leave to cool in the pans.

Once cool, remove the cakes from the pans. Place one of the cakes on a chopping board and cut out 5 circles of sponge with the cutter. Discard the trimmings (these can be crumbed and frozen for use in another recipe that calls for cake crumbs, such as cake pops or truffles). Repeat with the remaining 2 cakes.

Cut each small cake in half horizontally, so that you have

10 discs of cake in each colour, 30 in total.

To make the buttercream, whisk together the icing sugar, cream cheese, butter and lemon juice until you have achieved a smooth, stiff icing.

Spoon the buttercream into the piping/pastry bag and pipe a ring of buttercream around the edge of the 10 darkest purple cakes. Spoon a teaspoonful of the lavender lemon curd into the centre of each ring, then top

each with one of the light purple-coloured cakes. Repeat with another ring of buttercream and fill with lemon curd, then top each cake with one of the plain sponges. Dust the cakes with icing/confectioners' sugar, then decorate with the crystallized lavender flowers.

The stalks of the lavender are not edible, so these should be removed before eating.

These cakes will keep for up to 3 days stored in an airtight container, but are best eaten on the day they are made.

A BITCHY TEA
inspired by Cressida Cowper

Lemon balm tea

*Endive cups with Roquefort mousse,
pear & candied walnuts*

Feather cupcakes

Violet éclairs

Key lime trifle

Surly, churlish and thoroughly unpleasant, the discourteous debutante thinks nothing of bringing down her social-season rivals in a bid to snag the finest suitor. Too bad her RBF (resting bitch face) and snide remarks do nothing to ingratiate her to the gentlemen she's trying so hard to impress. After all of her scoffing at others, the ton's mean girl should take herself off to scoff her Bitchy Tea. There will be plenty of Roquefort mousse, light-as-a-feather cupcakes, violet éclairs and key lime trifle left over as she's unlikely to have any guests attending. More for her – just the way she likes it.

Lemon balm tea

A sour drink for the sour-faced one, perhaps if Cressida had been drinking this tasty tea when she was flirting with Colin, she'd have thought twice about wasting it by 'accidentally' spilling it all over Penelope.

3–4 teaspoons green or white tea leaves, or use the equivalent in tea bags

a small handful of fresh lemon balm leaves

honey or sugar, to taste

FOR 1 POT OF TEA

Warm the pot and add the tea. Add the lemon balm leaves and pour over boiled, slightly cooled water. Infuse for 5 minutes. Sweeten as desired.

Endive cups with Roquefort mousse, pear & candied walnuts

Ever the attention seeker, Cressida causes quite the scene when she swoons in front of the prince. The rich royal was alright... but these crunchy-yet-creamy bites are really something to swoon over.

1 tablespoon butter

60 g/¼ cup caster/white granulated sugar

140 g/1 cup walnut halves

125 g/4½ oz. Roquefort cheese

125 g/4½ oz. cream cheese

1 large ripe Anjou or Bartlett pear, peeled and finely diced

a little freshly squeezed lemon juice

20 small endive leaves, washed and patted dry

salt and freshly ground black pepper, to season

a baking sheet, greased

MAKES 20

First make the candied walnuts. Heat a non-stick pan/skillet over medium heat and add the butter, sugar and walnuts. Heat for about 5 minutes, stirring constantly until the sugar and butter have melted and the nuts are toasted and well coated in the mixture. Tip them onto the prepared baking sheet and quickly separate. Leave to cool.

Beat the Roquefort and the cream cheese together until blended and whipped. Season to taste with salt and pepper. Peel and finely dice the pear. Squeeze a little lemon juice over the dice.

To assemble, spoon a little blue cheese mousse into each endive cup, add a few pieces of diced pear and top each with a caramelized walnut.

Feather cupcakes

Eloise said, 'I've never understood the fashion for feathers in the hair. Why would a woman want to draw more notice to the fact that she's like a bird squawking for a man's attention in some bizarre ritual?' The squawking Cressida, with her elaborate hairdos, wholeheartedly disagrees.

500 g/1 lb. 2 oz. white sugarpaste
lilac food colouring paste
½ quantity Vanilla Buttercream (see page 20)
12 plain storebought cupcakes, ready to decorate
cornflour/cornstarch, for dusting
250 g/2 cups royal icing sugar
dark gold metallic food paint

a round cookie cutter the same size as the top of your cupcake
a piping/pastry bag fitted with a fine round nozzle/tip
a paintbrush

MAKES 12

Use a sharp knife to slice the top off of each cupcake horizontally to create a level surface. Next, spread a thin layer of buttercream over the top of each cupcake. Knead the sugarpaste with the lilac food colouring paste, adding a little at a time with a cocktail stick/toothpick. Roll out with a non-stick rolling pin on a clean (and lightly dusted with cornflour) work surface. Use the cookie cutter to stamp out discs and use these to cover the buttercream-coated cupcakes.

Mix up your royal icing according to the packet instructions, and fill your piping/pastry bag one-quarter full. Pipe a long line up the centre of your cupcake, with a slight curve in it, to form the central feather of your fan.

While the royal icing is still wet, take a dampened paintbrush and use this to smudge the lines of icing out. This should start to create a series of very fine lines of icing, which fill up a fluffy feather shape.

Repeat this process, piping lines to create a fan-shaped arrangement of feathers, all meeting in a point at the bottom edge. Finish your fan by piping a series of curved lines around the feathers to create a scalloped edge at the top of your fan, then brush this outwards, away from the feathers in the same way.

To finish, pipe a 'V' shape at the pointed edge of your fan. Allow the icing to dry for 10 minutes before painting with the gold food paint. Once dry, serve your art!

Violet éclairs

The beautiful climbing wisteria that decorates the Bridgerton's stately home – and shares a hue with these finger-licking éclairs – must be the envy of Cressida Cowper and her mother, the ultimate social climbers.

1 quantity Choux Pastry (see page 59)

FOR THE ICING

120 g/1 cup fondant icing/ confectioners' sugar, sifted

1 tablespoon violet-flavoured syrup or liqueur

purple food colouring

FOR THE FILLING

300 ml/2¼ cups double/heavy cream

1 tablespoon violet-flavoured syrup or liqueur

TO DECORATE

crystallized violets

a baking sheet, greased and lined
2 piping/pastry bags, 1 fitted with a large round nozzle/tip and 1 with a star nozzle/tip

MAKES 12

Preheat the oven to 200ºC (400ºF) Gas 6.

Spoon the choux pastry into the piping/pastry bag fitted with a round nozzle/tip and pipe 12 lengths of pastry, about 10 cm/4 inch long onto the baking sheet, a small distance apart. Pat down any peaks in the pastry using a clean wet finger.

Sprinkle a little water into the bottom of the oven to create steam which will help the choux pastry to rise.

Bake in the preheated oven for 10 minutes, then reduce the oven temperature to 180ºC (350ºF) Gas 4 and bake for a further 15–20 minutes until the pastry is crisp.

Remove from the oven and cut a small slit into each éclair with a sharp knife. Leave to cool.

Carefully cut each pastry in half horizontally using a sharp knife. For the icing, whisk together the icing sugar and violet syrup and a few drops of food colouring, if using, adding a few drops of water if necessary, and spread over the tops of the éclairs using a round-bladed knife. Decorate with the crystallized violets and leave to set.

For the filling, whisk together the cream and violet syrup until the cream reaches stiff peaks. Spoon into the piping/pastry bag fitted with a star nozzle/tip and carefully pipe a layer of cream into each éclair.

Cover with the iced tops and serve straight away or store in the fridge until needed.

These éclairs are best eaten on the day they are made.

Key lime trifle

Like this dessert, Ms Cowper is green (with envy). She should have known better than to trifle with Daphne, who warns her: 'You can either be a Duchess's friend, or her enemy.

FOR THE SPONGES

115 g/generous ½ cup caster/
  white granulated sugar

115 g/1 stick butter, softened

2 eggs

115 g/¾ cup plus 2 tablespoons
  self-raising/self-rising flour

1 tablespoon sour cream

finely grated zest of 2 limes

FOR THE KEY LIME MOUSSE

400-g/14-oz. can condensed milk

freshly squeezed juice of 6 limes

300 ml/1¼ cups double/heavy
  cream

FOR THE COOKIE CRUMB LAYER

300 g/10½ oz. ginger cookies

150 g/1¼ sticks butter, melted

FOR THE CURD

freshly squeezed juice of 2 limes

325 g/11½ oz. lime curd

green food colouring gel or paste
  (optional)

TO ASSEMBLE

300 ml/1¼ cups double/heavy
  cream

75 ml/5 tablespoons coconut rum
  (optional)

a 12-hole muffin pan, lined with
  muffin cases

a large glass dish

SERVES 8–10

Preheat the oven to 180ºC (350ºF) Gas 4.

For the sponges, whisk together the sugar and butter until light and creamy. Add the eggs one at a time, whisking well after each addition. Sift in the flour, and using a spatula gently fold in, along with the sour cream and the lime zest. Spoon the mixture into the paper cases in the muffin pan and bake in the oven for 20–25 minutes until the cupcakes are firm to touch and spring back when pressed with a clean finger.

Set aside to cool on a wire rack, then remove the paper cases. For the key lime mousse, add the condensed milk to a mixing bowl with the lime juice and whisk together. Add the double/heavy cream and whisk until the mixture starts to thicken.

For the cookie crumb layer, blitz the ginger cookies in a food processor to fine crumbs, then stir in the melted butter until all the crumbs are coated.

For the curd, whisk the lime juice into the lime curd, adding a little green food colouring gel if you wish. This will give the trifle a fun, vibrant colour, but it is for decoration only and is not absolutely necessary.

To assemble, whip the double cream to stiff peaks. Cut the sponges in half horizontally and place half of them cut-side up in the base of the glass dish.

Sprinkle over half of the rum, if using. Spoon over half of the condensed milk mixture and then cover with one-third of the cookie crumbs. Top with half of the curd.

Pour over the remaining condensed milk mixture and then top with the remaining halved sponge slices, drizzling with a little more rum, if using. Cover with the rest of the lime curd and half of the remaining crumbs and then top with the whipped cream.

Top with a final layer of the crumbs. Chill in the fridge for at least 3 hours before serving.

A CURIOUS TEA

inspired by Benedict Bridgerton

Earl Grey tea

Mini eggs 'Benedict'

Crackling brownie French fries

Tea voyage macarons

Passion fruit & chocolate layer cake

The second eldest son of the Bridgerton clan, nothing much is expected of Benedict in terms of societal duties. As such, he is free to explore his creativity, originality and sexuality... His shock when first introduced to the arty party scene by his friend Henry Granville is soon replaced with curiosity and enthusiasm. Indulge in this intriguing tea and ask yourself some of life's big questions: *Who am I? What do I want to be? How many slices of passion fruit chocolate cake is deemed appropriate?* A few nibbles on a crackling brownie French fry and you might just find yourself tempted towards the libertine lifestyle, too.

Earl Grey tea

With the lusty looks and flirty banter between Benedict and Henry, it's suggested that Benedict might be confused about who he desires. Does he want a lady or a lord, a countess or, indeed, an earl (grey)?

3 teaspoons Earl Grey tea leaves, or use equivalent in tea bags
sugar or honey, to taste

FOR 1 POT OF TEA

Warm the teapot and add the tea leaves. Pour over boiling water. Leave to brew for 5 minutes. Sweeten with sugar or honey, if desired.

~~~~~~

Mini eggs 'Benedict'

What's in a name? When you're a Bridgerton, rather a lot it seems! While Benedict can enjoy more freedom than his older brother Anthony, he sometimes has to walk on eggshells so as not to alarm his mother with his activities.

50 g/2 oz. can anchovy fillets, about 8, drained
60 ml/4 tablespoons milk
60 g/½ stick unsalted butter
a pinch of cayenne pepper
a pinch of ground nutmeg
a pinch of ground coriander
¼ teaspoon freshly squeezed lemon juice
8 quails' eggs
4 wafer-thin slices of wholemeal bread
2–3 tablespoons freshly chopped flat-leaf parsley
salt and freshly ground black pepper, to season

MAKES 16

Soak the anchovy fillets in the milk for about 10 minutes.

Drain the anchovy fillets and put them in a food processor with the butter, cayenne pepper, nutmeg, coriander, lemon juice and a good grinding of black pepper. Process until smooth and creamy.

Bring a saucepan of water to the boil, add the quails' eggs, then reduce the heat and simmer for about 4 minutes. Drain, then cover in cold water and let cool.

To serve, peel the eggs and cut in half lengthways. Toast the slices of bread until crisp and golden. Cut off and discard the crusts, then cut into quarters. Spread with a thin layer of anchovy relish, top with half a quail's egg and sprinkle with a little parsley. Serve immediately.

Crackling brownie French fries

When Benedict enters a new world of risqué soirées and adventurous art classes, he positively crackles with excitement. One bite of these fizzing fingers and so will you. Wonder what his policy is on double-dipping...

240 g/8½ oz. dark/bittersweet chocolate (55% cocoa), chopped

100 g/7 tablespoons butter, room temperature and cubed

120 g/⅔ cup caster/white granulated sugar

2 eggs

60 ml/¼ cup semi-skimmed milk

120 g/1 scant cup plain/all-purpose flour

25 g/¼ cup ground almonds/almond meal

1 teaspoon baking powder

1 vanilla bean

2 bags of popping candy, plus extra to serve

chocolate hazelnut spread, to serve

a 20-cm/8-inch square baking pan, greased and dusted with flour

MAKES 6–8

Preheat the oven to 190ºC (375ºF) Gas 5.

Put the chocolate in a heatproof bowl set over a saucepan of barely simmering water. Do not let the base of the bowl touch the water. Allow to melt, stirring occasionally, until completely smooth. Remove from the heat.

Put the butter in a bowl and beat with a wooden spoon until very soft. Beat in the sugar until well incorporated and creamy, then beat in one egg at a time. Add the milk and stir in. Add the flour, almonds and baking powder and beat in. Split the vanilla bean lengthways and scrape the seeds out into the bowl. Pour the melted chocolate in and add the popping candy. Mix everything together well. Spoon the mixture into the prepared baking pan, and spread level with a spatula. Bake in the preheated oven for about 15–20 minutes. Allow to cool in the pan for a few minutes, then turn out onto a wire rack to cool completely. Cut up the brownie into fat fries and serve with chocolate hazelnut spread for dipping in and extra popping candy for sprinkling over.

Tea voyage macarons

Benedict Bridgerton's journey of personal self-discovery involves a steamy threesome. As you're appreciating these 'three-part' macarons, smile at the thought of the top-hatted, cravatted one being undressed, then sandwiched between two beautiful women.

finely chopped pistachios, to sprinkle

TEA GANACHE

100 ml/⅓ cup plus 1 tablespoon single/light cream

50 g/2 oz. mascarpone

300 g/10½ oz. white chocolate, chopped

1 teaspoon butter

1 teaspoon matcha (green tea) powder

2 drops of pure jasmine extract

VANILLA MACARON SHELLS

240 g/1¾ cups icing/ confectioners' sugar

140 g/1½ cups ground almonds

½ vanilla bean

5 egg whites

50 g/¼ cup caster/superfine sugar

a piping/pastry bag, fitted with a plain nozzle/tip

baking sheets, greased and lined

MAKES ABOUT 25

Make the tea ganache the day before you want to bake the macarons. Put the cream and mascarpone in a saucepan and gently bring to the boil. Add the chocolate and butter and stir until melted. Remove from the heat and whisk with an electric whisk until smooth. Stir in the matcha powder and jasmine extract. Cover and refrigerate for 24 hours.

The next day, preheat the oven to 145ºC (275ºF) Gas 1. Bring the ganache to room temperature.

To make the vanilla macaron shells, sift the icing sugar into a food processor, add the almonds and blitz thoroughly. Split the vanilla bean lengthways and scrape the seeds out into a grease-free mixing bowl. Add the egg whites and whisk with an electric whisk until stiff peaks form. Gradually add the sugar, whisking until all the sugar is used up and the egg whites are glossy.

Fold the blitzed sugar and almonds into the egg whites until well combined and smooth. Fill the piping/pastry bag with the mixture and pipe neat 4-cm/1½-inch rounds on the prepared baking sheets. Space the rounds 3 cm/1¼ inches apart. Sprinkle a tiny amount of finely chopped pistachios on top of each round – not too much otherwise the macarons won't rise.

Allow to set for 30–60 minutes until a skin forms – you should be able to touch the surface of the macarons very gently with a wet finger without sticking to them. Bake in the preheated oven for about 12 minutes. Allow to cool on the baking sheet.

Fill the piping/pastry bag with the ganache and pipe some onto the flat underside of half of the cold macarons. Sandwich with another macaron shell. Refrigerate until ready to serve and eat within 7 days.

Passion fruit & chocolate layer cake

Revel in this naked cake, just as the newfound artist revels in drawing naked people. While there are four luscious layers to this sweet treat, now that the handsome Mr B's passion has been unleashed, there's no telling how many more layers of himself he'll reveal...

FOR THE CAKE MIXTURE

juice of 5 passion fruit, seeds removed

yellow food colouring

280 g/2½ sticks butter, softened

280 g/1½ cups caster/white granulated sugar

5 eggs

280 g/generous 2 cups self-raising/self-rising flour, sifted

2½ teaspoons baking powder

2½ tablespoons buttermilk or sour cream

FOR THE BUTTERCREAM

170 g/1¼ cups icing/confectioners' sugar, sifted

45 g/scant ½ cup unsweetened cocoa powder, sifted

45 g/3 tablespoons butter, softened

1 tablespoon milk

FOR THE GANACHE

80ml/⅓ cup double/heavy cream

100 g/3½ oz. plain/bittersweet chocolate

1 tablespoon butter

1 tablespoon golden/light corn syrup

FOR THE DECORATION

about 15 physalis

a food-safe, pesticide-free passion flower (optional)

two 20-cm/8-inch and two 10-cm/4-inch round cake pans, greased and lined

SERVES 12

Preheat the oven to 180ºC (350ºF) Gas 4.

For the cake mixture, use an electric whisk to mix the butter and sugar in a bowl until light and creamy. Add the eggs and whisk again. Fold in the flour, baking powder and buttermilk or sour cream using a spatula, until incorporated. Fold the passion fruit juice and a few drops of yellow food colouring into the cake batter.

Spoon the mixture into the prepared cake pans, dividing approximately two-thirds of the mixture between the 2 larger pans and the remaining one-third of the mixture between the 2 smaller pans. Bake the cakes in the preheated oven for 20–30 minutes, until golden brown and spring back to the touch and a knife inserted into the centre of each cake comes out clean. (The smaller cakes will take less time to cook than the larger ones, so check them towards the end of the cooking time.) Leave the cakes to cool in the pan for a few minutes, then turn out onto a wire rack to cool completely.

For the buttercream, whisk together the icing sugar, cocoa, butter and milk to a smooth, thick icing. For the ganache, put the cream, chocolate, butter and syrup in a heatproof bowl set over a pan of simmering water, making sure that the bottom of the bowl does not touch the water. Heat until the chocolate has melted, then stir everything together so that you have a smooth, glossy sauce.

To assemble, place one of the larger cakes on a serving plate. Spread approximately two-thirds of the buttercream over the top of the cake using a palette knife. Place the second large cake on top. Spread two-thirds of the ganache over the top. Place one of the smaller cakes in the centre of the large cakes. Spread the remaining buttercream over the top of the small cake and top with the final small cake. Cover the top cake with the remaining ganache in a thick layer.

To decorate the cake, place the physalis around the edge of the large cake and dust with icing sugar. Place the passion flower on top - it is for decoration only and should be removed before cutting the cake.

Never eat floral decorations unless certain it is safe to do so.

A FIRESIDE TEA
inspired by Violet Bridgerton

English breakfast tea
Warm Parmesan & bacon pancakes with chive butter
Toasted teacakes
Stem ginger cookies
Sticky marzipan & cherry loaf

Warm, comforting and traditional, just like this Fireside Tea, you know where you are with Violet Bridgerton. The glue that holds the Bridgerton family together, the calm, reassuring matriarch is dedicated to her children like only a loving mother can be. She'd think nothing of pouring a consoling cuppa, spreading a thick layer of butter onto a toasted teacake and cutting a sizeable slab of cherry loaf to serve her brood should they need a listening ear and a hug on a plate. If her tenderness and tasty treats are offered next to a toasty fire, so much the better. Flaming lovely.

English breakfast tea

A good, solid brew, this is the perfect beverage for Lady Bridgerton to offer her wise words of comfort and encouragement over.

3–4 teaspoons English Breakfast tea leaves or 2 tea bags
sugar, to taste
milk, as desired

FOR 1 POT OF TEA

Warm the pot. Add the tea and pour over boiling water. Leave to brew for 2–5 minutes. Sweeten to taste with sugar and add milk as desired.

~~~~~~

Warm Parmesan & bacon pancakes with chive butter

Bridgerton was set in the Regency era, when Parmesan ice cream was all the rage amongst the wealthy. Today, cheese ice cream sounds all kinds of wrong! These warm, cheesy pancakes are far more pleasingly palatable.

1 tablespoon vegetable oil, plus extra for brushing
3 strips of bacon, snipped into small pieces or 75 g/2½ oz. pancetta, cubed
115 g/¾ cup plus 2 tablespoons self-raising/self-rising flour
25 g/⅓ cup finely grated Parmesan cheese
a pinch of sea salt
1 egg, beaten
150 ml/⅔ cup full-fat/whole milk
salt and freshly ground black pepper, to season

FOR THE CHIVE BUTTER

85 g/6 tablespoons butter, at room temperature

2–2½ tablespoons snipped chives
salt and freshly ground black pepper, to season

MAKES ABOUT 20

To make the chive butter, put the butter in a bowl and beat in the chives. Season with salt and black pepper. Spoon the mixture into a ramekin or small serving bowl, cover and chill until needed.

Heat the oil in a large, non-stick frying pan/skillet and fry the bacon for about 3 minutes, until crispy. Remove from the pan and drain off any grease. Wipe the pan with paper towels and leave set over low heat.

Put the flour, cheese and salt in a large bowl and season well with pepper. Make a well in the middle. Add the egg and half the milk and gradually work in the flour to make a smooth batter. Beat in the remaining milk to make a smooth batter.

Drop tablespoonfuls of batter into the hot pan/skillet, sprinkle a little bacon on top and cook for 1–2 minutes, until bubbles appear on the surface. Flip over the pancake and cook for a further 30–60 seconds, until a golden colour.

Keep warm while you cook the remaining pancake batter. Serve hot with the pot of chive butter on the side, for spreading.

Toasted teacakes

Unlike other mothers in the ton, Violet doesn't need to 'butter up' would-be suitors for her lovely daughter Daphne; she trusts her to make her own decision and encourages her to marry for love. A toasted teacake, however, Lady Bridgerton will butter up with aplomb.

225 g/1⅔ cups strong white/bread flour

½ teaspoon sea salt

1 teaspoon easy-blend dried yeast

15 g/4 teaspoons light brown sugar

¼ teaspoon freshly grated nutmeg

60 g/½ cup mixed dried fruit

40 g/3 tablespoons butter, melted

120 ml/½ cup full-fat/whole milk, plus extra for brushing

butter, to serve

a baking sheet, greased

MAKES 8

Sift the flour, salt, yeast, sugar and nutmeg into a large bowl. Stir in the dried fruits and make a well in the centre.

Put the milk and butter in a small saucepan/skillet and heat until just warm.

Pour into the flour mixture and gradually work together to make a soft dough. Turn out onto a clean and lightly floured work surface and knead for about 5 minutes, until smooth and elastic. Place in a bowl, slip the bowl into a large plastic bag, seal with a rubber band and leave to rise for 1 hour, until doubled in size.

When risen, tip the dough out on to a lightly floured work surface, punch down, and divide into 8 pieces of equal size.

Shape each one into a ball, flatten slightly and arrange on the prepared baking sheet, spacing slightly apart. Slip the sheet into a large plastic bag and leave the dough to rise again for 45 minutes, until doubled in size.

Preheat the oven to 200°C (400°F) Gas 6.

Brush the top of each teacake with milk, then bake for about 15 minutes, until risen and golden and sounds hollow when the base is gently tapped. Transfer to a wire rack to cool. When ready to serve, split, toast on the cut sides and spread generously with butter.

Stem ginger cookies

With eight children (eight!), this strong, child-bearing machine may very well have benefitted from these zingy cookies during her pregnancies, as ginger is of course said to ease morning-sickness nausea...

85 g/¾ stick butter, at room temperature

75 g/6 tablespoons golden caster/white granulated sugar

1 egg yolk

½ teaspoon ground ginger

60 g/⅓ cup stem ginger in syrup (about 3 balls), chopped

25 g/¼ cup ground almonds/almond meal

115 g/¾ cup plus 3 tablespoons self-raising/self-rising flour

2 baking sheets, greased and lined

MAKES ABOUT 10

Preheat the oven to 160°C (325°F) Gas 3.

Beat the butter and sugar together until pale and creamy, then beat in the egg yolk. Stir in the ground ginger and stem ginger, then the ground almonds. Add the flour and mix well.

Roll the mixture into about 10 walnut-sized balls and arrange them on the prepared baking sheets, spacing well apart. Flatten slightly with your fingers and bake for about 20 minutes, until a pale golden brown colour.

Leave the cookies to cool on the baking sheets for a few minutes, until slightly firm, then use a spatula to transfer them to a wire rack to cool.

Sticky marzipan & cherry loaf

With cherry blossom trees forming a beautiful backdrop in the Bridgerton gardens, can't you just picture Violet sitting under one, nibbling on a slice of this sweet cake, whilst contemplating the goings-on inside her own extensive family tree?

175 g/¾ cup minus 2 teaspoons butter, at room temperature

175 g/¾ cup minus 2 tablespoons caster/white granulated sugar

3 eggs

175 g/1⅓ cups self-raising/ self-rising flour

85 g/¾ cup ground almonds/ almond meal

175 g/1¼ cups glacé/candied cherries, halved

75 g/2¾ oz. chilled marzipan, finely grated

icing/confectioners' sugar, for dusting

a 2-lb loaf tin, greased and lined

SERVES 8–12

Preheat the oven to 180ºC (350ºF) Gas 4.

Put the butter and sugar in a large bowl and beat until pale and creamy. Beat in the eggs one at a time. Sift in the flour and fold in, then stir in the cherries until evenly distributed in the mixture.

Spoon half the mixture into the prepared loaf tin and level the surface. Sprinkle with the grated marzipan. Top with the remaining mixture and smooth the surface.

Bake in the preheated oven for about 45 minutes, then remove the cake from the oven and cover the top with foil.

Return it to the oven and bake for a further 25 minutes, until risen and golden and a skewer inserted in the centre of the cake comes out clean. Leave the cake to cool in the tin for about 10 minutes, then lift out on to a wire rack to cool.

Serve the cake slightly warm or at room temperature.

Index

Dedication: For my great friend Susie, who burns for Bridgerton. KB

Senior Designers Geoff Borin & Toni Kay
Desk Editor Emily Calder
Head of Production Patricia Harrington
Art Director Leslie Harrington
Editorial Director Julia Charles
Publisher Cindy Richards
Writer Katherine Bebo
Illustrator Deanna Staffo
Indexer Vanessa Bird

First published in 2022 by Ryland Peters & Small
20–21 Jockey's Fields   341 E 116th St
London WC1R 4BW   New York NY 10029

www.rylandpeters.com

ISBN: 978-1-78879-431-2

10 9 8 7 6 5 4 3 2

MIX
Paper from responsible sources
FSC® C008047

Recipe collection compiled by Julia Charles and Emily Calder.
Recipe text © as listed opposite. Text by Katherine Bebo © Ryland Peters & Small 2022. Design and photography © Ryland Peters & Small 2022. Illustrations © Deanna Staffo 2022.

A CIP record for this book is available from the British Library. US Library of Congress CIP data has been applied for.

Printed and bound in China

Notes
• Both British (Metric) and American (Imperial) are given for your convenience. It is important to work with one set of measurements and not alternate within a recipe.

• All eggs are medium (UK) or large (US) unless specified as large, in which case US extra-large should be used.

• Floral decorations should only be consumed if the are food safe – always check before using.

RECIPE CREDITS

Kiki Bee: Chocolate liquor pudding; Kiss & tell tarts. **Mickael Benichou**: Bijoux blondies; Crackling brownie french fries; Garden cupcakes; Praline cookies; Tea voyage macarons; White chocolate & rose cookies. **Susannah Blake:** Angel food cake; Baby rarebits with beetroot/beet & orange relish; Boiled eggs with asparagus 'dippers'; Champagne cocktails; Chocolate pecan cookies; Creamy tomato & mascarpone tartlets with grilled artichokes; Dark chocolate floral cake; Drop scones with cinnamon butter; Finger sandwiches; Lavender shortbread; Love heart sugar cookies; Meringues with rosewater cream; Mini croque-monsieurs; Mini eggs 'Benedict'; Raspberry & lemon Mille-feuilles; Rich fruit cake; Rosemary scones with cream cheese & Parma ham; Smoked mackerel pâté on toast; Stem ginger cookies; Sticky marzipan & cherry loaf; Strawberry sables; Teatime crostini; Toasted teacakes; Topped cornbread toasts; Tropical tea punch; Warm Parmesan & bacon pancakes with chive butter.
Julia Charles: Endive cups with Roquefort mousse, pear & candied walnuts. **Linda Collister:** Espresso brownies. **Lydia France:** Buffalo mozzarella, pickled fig & lemon crostini. **Liz Franklin:** Caramelized fennel & prawn/shrimp polenta crostini; Earl Grey tea; English breakfast tea; Formosa oolong tea; Fraises-des-bois friands; Fresh spinach & herb frittata; Ginger & honey tea; Ginger tea; How to make tea; Jasmine flowering tea; Lapsang souchong tea; Lemon balm tea; Lemon drizzle cake; Moroccan mint tea; Rooibos red tea; Rose congou tea; Rosemary & Asiago arancini; Tippy green tea; Yunnan tea.
Laura Gladwin: The Featherington martini. **Victoria Glass:** Chocolate & hazelnut biscotti; Mulled wine chocolate wreath; Opera cake.
Jane Mason: Fruit Buns. **Hannah Miles:** Chouquettes; Croquembouche; Heart choux buns; Key lime trifle; Lady Grey tea cake; Lemon & lavender cakes; Mini ice cream cakes; Passion fruit & chocolate layer cake; Peach melba scones; Rose & raspberry choux rings; Spanish Windtorte; Violet éclairs. **Annie Rigg:** Macarons.
Angela Romeo: Cherry & pistachio cupcakes; Fallen fruit chocolate cake; Fig & pistachio cupcakes. **Janet Sawyer:** Lemon syllabub.
Will Torrent: 'Coronation' chicken sandwiches with pickled red onion; Crab mayonnaise éclairs. **Bea Vo:** Lemon verbena semolina cookies; Raspberry meringues. **Charlotte White:** Chocolate cherry cake; Feather cupcakes.

PHOTOGRAPHY CREDITS

Martin Brigdale: Pages 1, 8, 11, 14, 16, 39–46, 58, 62, 64, 66, 86, 89, 90, 92, 94, 97, 103-109, 112, 126, 135–141. **Peter Cassidy:** 114. **Jean Cazals:** 32. **Dan Jones:** 36, 82, 85. **Mowie Kay:** 73. **Adrian Lawrence:** 26, 52. **William Lingwood:** 17, 51, 78, 100. **Steve Painter:** 29, 35, 49, 57, 61, 68, 71, 76, 91, 98, 110, 116, 124, 129–132. **Matt Russell:** 81. **Kate Whitaker:** 18, 23–25, 55, 65, 74, 101, 123. **Isobel Wield:** 2, 3, 9, 10, 12, 13, 19, 30, 120. **Clare Winfield:** 21, 119.